Don't Call Me Inspirational

HARILYN ROUSSO

Don't Call Me Inspirational

A Disabled Feminist Talks Back

Temple University Press ⊤ Philadelphia

TEMPLE UNIVERSITY PRESS
Philadelphia, Pennsylvania 19122
www.temple.edu/tempress

Library of Congress Cataloging-in-Publication Data

Rousso, Harilyn, 1946–
   Don't call me inspirational : a disabled feminist talks back /
Harilyn Rousso.
      p. cm.
   ISBN 978-1-4399-0936-2 (cloth : alk. paper) —
ISBN 978-1-4399-0937-9 (pbk. : alk. paper) —
ISBN 978-1-4399-0938-6 (e-book)   1. Rousso, Harilyn,
1946–   2. Women with disabilities—United States—Biography.
3. Feminists—United States—Biography.   4. People with
disabilities—United States—Psychology.   5. Discrimination
against people with disabilities—United States.   I. Title.
   HV3013.R68A3 2013
   362.4092—dc23
   [B]
                                          2012025882

Printed in the United States of America

082713P

In loving memory of my parents,

Evelyn and David Rousso;

my partner Gene Brown's parents,

Estelle and Morton Brown;

and my sister-in-law, Judy Rousso

Contents

Preface

When I began writing the pieces that became the chapters of this book, I had no intention of writing a book, much less a memoir. My mother had recently died after a lengthy illness. While she was ill, she had turned into an unhappy, angry person with little resemblance to the strong, feisty woman who had had such a powerful, positive influence on my life. I started writing about her in an attempt to recapture that spirited mother of my childhood. Through those early pieces, my familiar, strong-willed mother reappeared and began once again, for better or worse, to reassert her influence on me. I found writing very healing, and I learned a great deal about the power of words to capture and transform both the past and the present.

Once I realized what was happening, I became hooked on writing, and I began exploring other issues in my life that elicited strong emotions—shame, pain, anger, and frustration, as well as joy and humor. Over time, I found that I was writing increasingly about my feelings and attitudes about being a woman with a disability, and I realized how much these feelings had changed over the course of my life. I had grown up denying my disability but had come to embrace it as a source of positive identity and community; as a young adult I had doubted my womanhood, but I now declared myself a feminist. While I intuitively understood many of the factors that contributed to these changes, I did not reflect on them deeply until I began writing. Writing became a means of reflecting, recording, and, in some cases, revealing to myself my deepest secrets. In conjunction with my work as an activist and an artist, it became another way to confront the prejudice and discrimination I had faced as a disabled woman.

After I had been writing about my experiences for many years, a participant in one of the writing workshops I was attending suggested that I had a book on my hands. I was first surprised and then anxious—do I really want to reveal so much of myself? Eventually, I became hopeful that some of my experiences might speak to others. In part because of the way this book evolved and in part because of my temperament, my story does not unfold chronologically. As a visual artist, I think about the book as a collage or series of images about my life rather than a formal portrait. The first chapter orients the reader with an overview of my life's journey, and the remaining chapters are loosely gathered into five thematic sections: attitudes toward disability, family, body image, views of womanhood, and activism. Readers who are so inclined are welcome to create their own collage, reading sections and chapters out of sequence, more or less the way I wrote them.

Acknowledgments

I owe my first thanks to my writing instructors, Bea Gates, Charles Salzberg, and Nancy Kelton, who enabled me to grow as a writer and to "give birth" to this book. Bea read several drafts of the manuscript and was an ongoing source of support and wisdom. Charles facilitated the publication of some of my pieces and read a later draft of the manuscript. In Nancy's workshops, I wrote the earliest pieces in the book and got hooked on writing. A fellow workshop member, Lucy Field Goodman, was the first person to suggest that I had the makings of a book. Cathy McCandless, John Masterson, Robert Penn, and my longtime friends Linda Marks and Paula Webster all offered thoughtful comments that strengthened the work.

Katinka Neuhof and Robert Roth, both fine writers and good friends, read the manuscript with great care and kindness, providing excellent suggestions and advice. Robert also helped me secure opportunities to participate in readings.

I did much of my writing in the Writers Room, an urban writers' colony in New York City, where I participated in one of my first readings of this work; as a result, one of the members, Karol Nielsen, encouraged me to submit a piece to *Epiphany, a Literary Journal*, which went on to publish it. Chapter 21 is a modified version of that essay, which was previously published as Harilyn Rousso, "On Not Looking in the Mirror," *Epiphany, a Literary Journal* (Spring/Summer 2010): 103–105. David Evanier's reaction to my reading, "You should be published," was timely and very meaningful to me. Executive Director Donna Brodie also offered strong encouragement.

Modified versions of other chapters have been previously published as well. Chapter 2 was previously published as Harilyn Rousso, "Birth, Mine," *ducts*, no. 4 (Summer 2000), available at http://www.ducts.org/06_00/toc_frameset.html. Chapter 20 was previously published as Harilyn Rousso, "Walk Straight and Die," *ducts*, no. 5 (Fall 2000), available at http://www.ducts.org/09_00/

toc_frameset.html. Chapter 30 was previously published as Harilyn Rousso, "Buying the Wedding Dress," *ducts*, no. 7 (Summer 2001), available at http://www.ducts.org/06_01/memoirs/rousso .html, and as Harilyn Rousso, "Buying the Wedding Dress," in *How Not to Greet Famous People: The Best Stories from ducts.org*, ed. J. Kravetz and C. Salzberg, 63–64 (Kearney, NE: Morris, 2004).

I am also grateful to William L. Andrews, Ellen Bravo, Julie Enszer, Beth Ferri, Michelle Fine, Anne Finger, Jonathan Kravetz, Laurie Lehman, Lynne Rienner, Mary Severance, Sunny Taylor, and Michael L. Wehmeyer for their support and advice.

Members of my creativity group, which has been meeting for almost twenty years—Nancy Barnes, Diane Goodstein, and Linda Marks—provided support, advice, humor, common sense, and (I hesitate to say this) "inspiration." Thank you, dear sisters.

Some of my other sisters, those in the disability community, who helped sustain me include Nadina LaSpina, with whom I met regularly to commiserate and celebrate our commitment to writing memoirs; Simi Linton, who cajoled and convinced me that getting published was possible; Anna Fay, Roberta Galler, Bobbi Linn, and Corbett O'Toole, who also encouraged me and allowed me to write about our friendship; and Cynthia Collazo, Patricia Fraser, Kelly Irish, Ione Lewis, Manyon Lyons, and Djuna Parmley Wilson, younger disabled women who were willing to reflect on their experiences with the Networking Project. I also owe a world of gratitude to Betty Bock, who—as the first woman with a disability that I allowed into my life—helped me begin to embrace my disability identity. I deeply appreciate the disability rights movement as a whole, which had a profound influence on my life; without it, I might still view disability as a defect rather than an asset.

My dear friends Debra Shabas and Richard Heller deserve a thank-you and a hug for more than ten years of love and all kinds of support and advice, both informal and professional. Similarly, Adrienne Asch, Sally Brown, Beth Cohen, Rosemarie Garland-Thomson, Lula Gaskins, Carol Gill, Aviva Gold, Claire Harnan, Judy Heumann, Sue Klein, Kathy Martinez, Linda Nessel, Sally Nystrom, Angela Perez, Carol Ann Roberson, Ellen Rubin, Ellen

Wahl, and Leslie R. Wolfe have enriched my life with their friendship. I also thank the members of my women's consciousness-raising group, who began my transformation into a feminist. And special thanks go to Gloria Steinem, who taught me through her actions the true meaning of sisterhood and feminism.

Janet Francendese at Temple University Press has been an amazingly perceptive reader and editor, with an extraordinary grasp of my issues as a disabled woman; at times she seemed to know me better than I knew myself. I also greatly appreciate the help and support of others at the press, including Amanda Steele, assistant editor; Joan Vidal, senior production editor; and Gary Kramer, publicity manager. In addition, I am grateful to Rebecca Logan, project manager at Newgen, who provided invaluable assistance on production aspects of the book.

My first community was my family—my parents, Evelyn and David Rousso; my sister, Sandy Izhakoff; and my brother, Eli Rousso. Without their loving support and total confidence in me, I most likely would have had a different, far more limited life and there would have been no book for me to write. I especially thank my mother for teaching me how to talk back.

Finally, there are not enough words to describe my love for and gratitude to my partner, Gene Brown. A highly accomplished writer with an extensive list of publications, he walked with me through each step of the book-writing process, doggedly hanging in there even when I was kicking and screaming. He read and edited every version of every chapter and offered sound advice on query letters, proposals, titles, and everything else. This book would not have come to life without him. He is and will always remain the love and the light of my life.

I

Close Encounters with the Clueless

1. Who's Harilyn?

I am a sixty-six-year-old woman with cerebral palsy. I was named after my maternal grandfather, Harry; when I turned out to be a girl rather than the boy everyone expected, my parents made up the name "Harilyn" in his honor. I could have done worse; everyone remembers my name. I was born and raised in New York City, and I still live there, in Greenwich Village. I am a college graduate with advanced training in social work and psychotherapy. But most of the work I have done over the past twenty-five years is as a disability rights activist. I advocate for and educate others on the needs, rights, and abilities of people with disabilities. I have a "significant other," Gene Brown, a smart, charming, loving man whom I have been with for more than twenty-five years. In addition to working and spending time with my partner, I like to paint and write. I also love crime shows on TV.

I want to tell you what it means to me to have a disability, cerebral palsy, and to describe my journey from "passing"—that is, pretending I wasn't disabled—to embracing my disability as an acceptable and (on a good day) even positive part of myself. Cerebral palsy (or CP) is a disability affecting body movements and coordination. Doctors have said I have a "mild" case of cerebral palsy, I suppose because I don't use assistive devices or need much help with daily tasks. Nonetheless, my CP affects the way I walk, move, hold my body, and speak. My walk is off-balance and, in my mind, ungraceful. Because I have a fair amount of involuntary movement in my arms and hands, pouring liquids, cutting on a straight line, and doing other tasks that require a lot of coordination and precision are extremely difficult for me to achieve. You wouldn't want me as your brain surgeon. However, I can write, paint, cook, and do most of what I need to do to get through the day. My speech is somewhat strained; it is usually comprehensible after people listen to me for a while. But when I'm tired or upset, my speech can sound quite garbled. When I speak, I often make weird facial gestures in an effort to get my words out, so my disability is definitely visible and noticeable. Particularly when I was a kid, I faced a lot of staring and pointing and stupid questions like "What's wrong with you?" which I hated. I still face stares and questions, but they usually bother me less, depending on my mood. Sometimes I stare back or say something provocative like "Nothing wrong with me. What's *your* problem?" I like the idea of giving ignorant people a dose of their own medicine.

I grew up denying that I had cerebral palsy or any kind of disability. I did not want to be seen as different or, more to the point, defective. Of course, I knew I had differences—that I walked and talked differently. I just didn't want to own up to them. I was afraid that if I said I had a disability, I'd be rejected and excluded; whereas, if I kept my mouth shut and pretended I was "normal," no one would notice. It was a fantasy I held on to for a long time. I think the fact that I had CP rather than another type of disability made me even more eager to deny it. Cerebral palsy is not a very sexy disability; to me, it seemed downright disgusting.

My mother did volunteer work for an organization that helped children who were more significantly disabled as the result of CP than I was. They had not only greater physical limitations but also what I call "CP mannerisms"—shaking limbs, difficult-to-understand speech, weird facial expressions, drooling—that were more pronounced than mine. Looking at these children was like looking at myself in one of those distorted mirrors in a house of horrors. I was afraid that I was as ugly and repulsive as they seemed to me. Also, many of the children had what was then called mental retardation and is now called intellectual disabilities. I prided myself in being smart, and I was fearful that if I said I had CP, people would think I was a "retard." (Actually, some kids at school called me that anyway.) The people with CP that I saw where my mother volunteered seemed like they couldn't have much of a life. I assumed that no one would love them, so they'd never get married or have children, and that they would never be able to go to school or find a job. They seemed not quite human to my insecure mind. I couldn't bear the thought of being like them. Not me. I was okay. I was "normal."

My denial made me refuse to learn anything about CP. I didn't want to know about CP because I didn't want to have it. And I didn't want to get to know anyone who had CP or any other disability. I wanted to be left alone and to be like everyone else.

I've come a long way since then. At this point in my life, most of the time I feel fine about having CP. I can't say I love it, but I don't hate it either. It's more a fact of my life that I live with comfortably and that, when the situation arises, I can speak about fairly openly without shame or apology. At times, particularly in recent years, I have come to view my disability as a positive source of identity and community. That's not to say that I don't occasionally encounter someone with CP—or even see myself in the mirror—and freak out. But those freak-outs don't happen nearly as often as they used to. I'll share with you some of what helped me move past my denial and self-hate.

When I was in my late twenties, after a lifetime of avoidance of other people with CP or any other disability, I decided it was time to start meeting others who were disabled. My motivation was self-serving. I had decided to become a psychotherapist and thought that I might be able to build up my own business as a therapist, or what is called in the trade a "private psychotherapy practice," by working with people with disabilities. In hindsight, it was an absurd plan. I was so conflicted about my own disability that it was ridiculous to think I could help others with disabilities, especially if they were coming to therapy to resolve disability issues. Also, disabled people seeking psychotherapy wouldn't necessarily want a disabled therapist. For a host of reasons, including their own hang-ups about disability, they might simply prefer a nondisabled, "normal" therapist. But I was naïve and didn't know how impractical my plan was, so I just went full speed ahead.

I was lucky in the sense that I began exploring my disability identity in the late 1970s, when the disability rights movement was gaining strength. People with disabilities, influenced by the civil rights movement and the women's movement, realized that they, too, faced discrimination and began organizing for equal rights. At that time, disability rights groups were forming in New York City and in most major cities throughout the country. These groups seemed like the perfect place for me to meet people with disabilities and "drum up business" for my psychotherapy practice. I began attending meetings of one of the earliest and most successful disability rights groups in New York City, Disabled in Action, and was amazed to find people there who had disabilities *and* were smart, attractive, and fun to be with. I became close friends with several people with disabilities, including a few with CP, who, unlike me, talked openly about being disabled. When I began to follow their example and share my feelings about my disability, I was initially frightened but also greatly relieved. I didn't have to pretend I was nondisabled any more. And, for the first time, I was not the only one in the group with a disability. My new friends understood firsthand my disability experiences and didn't judge or abandon me.

In the midst of my meeting these new friends with disabilities, something important happened in my career that helped me, or maybe I should say forced me, to embrace my identity as a person with a disability still further. As I mentioned, I had decided to become a psychotherapist, and after obtaining a master's degree in social work, I had enrolled in a psychotherapy institute to get more training. When I had been at that institute for about a year, I was asked to leave on the grounds that some of the key staff thought that a person with my disability could not be a good psychotherapist. The administrators were convinced that my CP mannerisms would distress my psychotherapy clients, causing them to flee—or at least to ask for another, more "normal" therapist.

I was horrified by the staff's decision to expel me. I had never before faced such obvious discrimination. I knew it was wrong for others to use my disability to deny me opportunities. It was like denying someone a job because he was African American or because she was a woman. That was discrimination based on prejudice, and prejudice was not right, especially in this country, which was supposed to provide equal opportunity for all. By way of the experience of being asked to leave the institute, I came to understand more fully than ever before that many of the problems I was facing in my life—the rejection, the staring, the isolation—were caused not by my disability, my CP, but by prejudice against my disability. And I had to recognize that I, too, was prejudiced— I held many of the same negative stereotypes about my disability as the staff at the institute and the world at large. That was why I had to deny my disability—because, at that time, I thought that to claim it would mean that I had accepted those stereotypes as *the* truth about me. Of course, the stereotypes were wrong, but until I was thrown out of the institute, I never questioned them.

Recognizing my own prejudice was a real revelation. While I wasn't suddenly able to claim my disability with pride, I was able to understand that my reluctance to acknowledge having a disability was not the fault of my disability itself but rather the fault of my attitude toward it. So the question was this: How do I change my attitude?

After I left the institute, I took several steps that helped. First, I looked for other therapists with disabilities to learn what their experiences had been. Many of the more than forty that I tracked down told me that they, too, had faced discrimination in both their training and their careers as psychotherapists. After sharing our experiences, we decided to raise awareness of disability discrimination in our area of work. We formed a group of psychotherapists with disabilities, organized a conference on disability discrimination in the psychotherapy profession, and wrote a paper about the conference that was published in a major mental health journal. In addition, with support from the other disabled therapists, I decided to sue the institute that had expelled me, charging them with disability discrimination. Even though I did not win the lawsuit, because disability rights laws at that time were not as strong as they are today, the very process of filing the lawsuit was empowering. I felt like I was taking action rather than allowing myself to be a passive victim of discrimination. All of these acts caused me to become very public about the fact that I had a disability. I could no longer hide in the closet or deny that I had CP—nor did I want to. I was out there—and I had a community that provided support and solidarity.

Now that I identified as disabled, I became involved in fighting for the rights of people with disabilities as part of my work life. For example, I started a program for adolescent girls with disabilities, providing them with the opportunity to meet adult women with disabilities who served as mentors and role models. I wrote and spoke extensively about issues of disability. Yet I continued to grapple with mixed feelings about my disability. I had grown up thinking that disabled people were defective, abnormal, even freaks, and although I now knew better, at least intellectually, it was hard for me to shake those old notions. For example, I was often surprised when I unexpectedly caught a glimpse of myself in a store window or in a mirror and saw that I had those CP mannerisms. Despite my disability activism, somewhere in my head I still saw myself as nondisabled. Also, I continued to feel uneasy when I encountered some people with CP. They, too, served as mirrors, challenging that image of myself as "normal."

Such grappling continued for years—decades, in fact—and I'm not entirely comfortable with my disabled body even today. But other experiences, besides disability activism, helped me progress in the process of truly embracing myself as a woman with CP. First, I fell in love. Or more to the point, a few men whom I wanted fell in love with me—not all at once, mind you, but at different points in my life. During my adolescence and young adulthood, I had never dated. I simply assumed that no man would want me, given my disability. I finally began dating in my late twenties, a time of my life when I was feeling successful in my work, had my own apartment, and felt it was time to get out of my cocoon and at least "try" to date. So I joined some social clubs, wrote some personal ads in newspapers, and hoped for the best. I was still terrified, and naïve—I didn't even know how to kiss or neck, much less have sex—but I was determined to put myself out there. I discovered that dating was not as impossible as I had thought. Sure, lots of men were turned off by my disability, but not all men were. And, best of all, a few were interested and actually turned on. To become romantically involved with men who found me attractive, desirable, and sexy with my body, disability and all, was very healing. Their appreciation of my body just the way it was helped me appreciate and see it through their eyes.

In a related but less dramatic way, the appreciation of my disabled body by some of my women friends also helped me develop a more positive body image. For example, when I complained about my clumsy, unfeminine walk to one of my closest friends, who had a disability herself, she said, "I love to see your 'crooked' walk, because when I see it, it means you are coming to visit." To my friends, my disability, including my CP mannerisms, were just part of the person they liked very much; their more positive associations with respect to my mannerisms helped me challenge my more negative associations.

Another factor that helped me challenge my negative feelings about my disabled body was my own psychotherapy. I was not only a psychotherapist but also, for many years, a patient in psychotherapy. One of the most helpful things that my therapist did was to encourage me to be curious about my negative feelings toward my body. At one point in my treatment, he suggested that instead of my sitting in a chair facing him, I lie on a couch, which is typical in a deeper form of psychotherapy. When you are lying down, you can't see the therapist's reactions to what you are saying, so you can become more involved in your own thoughts and feelings. I was reluctant to lie on the therapist's couch because I have a harder time controlling my bodily movements when I'm reclining. When I explained my hesitation to my therapist, he asked why I cared if I shook more. At first, I thought that was a ridiculous question. Surely most people would be self-conscious if they had involuntary movements that they couldn't control. But I was wrong. He explained that while my involuntary movements were indeed a fact about my body, I could have many different kinds of feelings about that fact. For example, I could hate the movements and feel ashamed, love them and feel proud, or not have strong feelings one way or the other. That there were many ways that I could feel about my body was a revelation that gave me hope. I realized that while I couldn't change the facts about my disability, perhaps I could change the feelings. Of course, I knew that already from my experiences with activism, romance, and friendships, which had all shifted my feelings about my disability. But my therapist's simple formulation—facts versus feelings about facts—and his curiosity about why I felt negative rather than some other way gave me a greater understanding and sense of control over my feelings. Perhaps I didn't have to rely solely on the disability community, on friends, on lovers, or even on therapists to nudge my feelings along. Maybe I could take a more active stance on my own.

In the past few years, I have been trying to figure out how to further shift my attitude toward my disability in a positive direction. For example, I've used my interest in making art, specifically painting. I took up painting in my forties—I was a late bloomer—because I felt a strong desire to express myself nonverbally. Words often felt too confining and controlled. I was eager to let loose.

As an experiment, I took a few painting classes, and I loved them. I found that my shaky hands were not necessarily a liability; at times they were an asset, enabling me to feel free and spontaneous. At first I didn't give much thought to what I wanted to paint, but over time my work has become increasing autobiographical, depicting my disabled body and my life as a disabled woman.

In some paintings I have focused on the parts of my body that looked most different from the norm. For example, I have limited use of my right hand, and my fingers not only have a great deal of involuntary movement but also turn up, so they look like a bunch of small bananas. I've always been self-conscious about this hand because it looks weird. I have made several big paintings of this hand that capture the odd shape of my fingers. The very process of painting my hand has changed my attitude toward it. First, I have fallen in love with some of the colors and textures that I've used to create the hand on paper. The image has been transformed from an oddity to a colorful, beautiful form—a piece of art. Second, the large size of the image creates a sense of power; my weak little hand, which in daily life seems unable to do much, in the picture becomes a symbol of strength. Finally, that hand, with its odd twists and turns, is recognizably, undeniably mine—it's me, like a self-portrait. There's something endearing and appealing about seeing it up on the easel or wall. As a result of these paintings of my hand, I've come to like my real right hand better—my feelings have shifted.

I've also made collages that consist of cut-up photographs of my face, specifically my mouth. When I talk, the muscles around my mouth get tight and can create facial expressions that are quite scary. I have captured some of those frightening expressions in photos and have deliberately included them in the collages, along with other, more flattering facial photos. Placed in collages, those scary images become less scary and more interesting. They become part of abstract patterns of light and dark and shape that make me want to look rather than turn away. So when I see my "scary" expressions in the mirror, I remember the collages and I can see the movements of my mouth in another, more positive way.

Writing is another way I work on my feelings about my CP. I have written about those parts of myself that I dislike the most. Describing these parts in great detail has become a form of knowing and claiming them. Yet I often struggle to find words that are free of judgment. For example, in describing my walk, I find myself using negative words such as *awkward, off-balance, crooked,* and *ungraceful.* My mixed feelings about my body influence my choice of words. I cannot come up with descriptions that are less biased. I am hopeful that if or when my feelings shift to a more neutral or positive stance, my words will shift in the same direction.

In addition to writing descriptions about my bodily features, I've written about how I deal with feeling like a freak (I consider a religious ritual called an exorcism to evict the freakish feelings), how I handle being stared at (I stare back while harboring murderous fantasies), and what the advantages are of having a wandering right hand (it can be very useful in sexual activities). Essentially I've been trying to write about as many aspects of my disability experience as I can think of, both good and bad, in part so I can stop having secrets from myself about my disability and so I can develop a more balanced view of what having a disability, specifically CP, has meant in my life.

Having a disability has helped shape some important parts of my identity that I value—like being open to differences of all kinds in other people (I'm often more open to others' differences than to my own), like being a fighter for social justice (any type of prejudice or discrimination infuriates me), and like having a knack for creative problem solving (you have to become creative when you can't do things in the usual ways).

I have not yet fully owned my disability, but I'm in a better place than I was even last year, and definitely better than five years ago. I have more work to do on the road to self-discovery and self-acceptance, and I will probably come across some tools that I haven't yet tried or even thought of—like belly dancing or flying a plane. I need to keep discovering new ways to be out there in the world as myself, with myself, with no need to cover up or pretend.

I'm betting on the fact that ultimately, being exactly who I am, a woman with CP, will give me the best shot at having the kind of life I want. Definitely it will give me the most energy for creating a good life. Covering up my disability identity has zapped a lot of energy that could be used for more important endeavors, like painting or falling in love.

So that's my story, my journey in a nutshell. Having come to a place where I not only accept but at times appreciate and celebrate my disability status, I'd like to offer support and a bit of advice to young people who may be struggling with the fact that they have a disability and who may be hoping beyond hope that it will go away or that no one will notice. I'd like them to consider the possibility that they can stop hiding and pretending, that they can claim disability and be all right. There's no magic pill to get them to that all-right place—if there were, I'd gladly give it to them (and take one myself). But there is a path, their path, to get there. Maybe my journey will help them. Even if nothing I did makes any sense to them and they have to forge their own direction, I want them to take heart. They should trust themselves to find their way—and call on some of their older sisters and brothers with disabilities to help them. Most important, they should know that there are some great moments of self-discovery and freedom ahead of them.

Daring to claim disability or any part of yourself that you have been taught to disavow can be an amazing adventure, as you are about to see.

2. Birth, Mine

I was in a hurry to be born. When my mother began experiencing intense labor pains, my father whisked her to the hospital, but her doctor had not yet arrived—he was "en route," a euphemism for nobody knowing where he was. Then, as now, I would wait for no man and began giving all the telltale signs that I was about to emerge. But the nurses were not having it. They could not allow a birth to occur without the doctor present, and he still was nowhere to be found. To keep me under control, the nurses pushed my mother's legs shut, which greatly limited my ability to peek out into the world, not to mention my ability to breathe. My mother reports scratching and biting the nurses, fearful that their delaying tactics were not good for my health. She was right, of course, but that would not be known for some time. My mother complained bitterly to the doctor when he finally arrived, but he insisted no harm had been done. In fact, I appeared to be all right when I was allowed to be born, a large and seemingly sturdy baby with a full head of dark brown hair.

My eagerness to embrace the world continued throughout my infancy, for I was a very curious baby. Yet I was slow to crawl and walk, and my eye-hand coordination left a lot to be desired. The visits to specialists began early. My mother's own doctor was convinced she was neurotic, imagining delays in my development where there were none, but my mother persisted. She heard more than her share of double-talk from doctors, including from one so-called pediatric expert, who after seeing me for a few minutes when I was nine months old, was fully convinced that I had a hole in my head and should be immediately institutionalized. It was my good fortune that my mother paid him no mind. She knew something was wrong but not that wrong. Not until I was three years old did the accurate diagnosis emerge: cerebral palsy as the result of insufficient oxygen at birth. There had been damage to the part of my brain affecting coordination and motor control. My disability was relatively mild, and the diagnosing doctor advised my mother to raise me as a "normal" child, but no one in my family had ever been accused of being normal, and I was not going to be the first.

I am grateful for the delayed diagnosis; it allowed the family legend about my birth to take hold. My mother repeated the story of my impatience to be born hundreds of times throughout her life, never with regret, only with pride. She would not let on until I was fully grown how guilty she felt about my birth trauma, guilt that was clearly unwarranted. Actually, by biting and scratching those nurses, she began her career as my advocate even before I was born. I, in turn, learned how to bite and scratch on my own behalf and for others. I never have allowed myself to think of how I must have felt when I was nearly suffocated just at the moment of emergence. Or how my life might have been transformed had I been in less of a hurry. I have thought most about my determination to be born and to claim my place in the world. It is an image of a doer and an activist, never a victim. Yet at times it has been a difficult legacy.

I remember when I was five years old, moving to a new home in Queens with my mother; father; older brother, Eli; and older sister, Sandy. It was my parents' first house on a tree-lined street, two stories high and a backyard with swings and a wormy peach tree. Family pictures show me as a cute five-year-old with a pixie haircut and a winning smile. But there was no question that I walked and talked funny. My legs and toes turned in, causing me to trip over my own feet with regularity; my speech, though comprehensible, was slurred, suggesting sleepiness or drunkenness, depending on your perspective. The day my family moved in, I sat on the curb on one side of the street, and six neighborhood children my age sat on the other side of the street, just staring. One little girl began giggling and whispering to the girl next to her, pointing to my ugly brown high-ankle shoes with heavy laces that seemed more suitable for boys than girls. Later, another girl, Sally, crossed the street and said to me, "I'll be your friend. The other kids won't want to be friends with you. You're crippled." "No thanks; I can make lots of friends," I said with a sense of assurance that I sometimes envy today. At that age I didn't feel all that different, much less "crippled." I knew I moved clumsily, but that was just the way I was since birth. After all, my legs got me where I wanted to go, and I could play ball and hopscotch, albeit in my own way. And I loved chocolate ice-cream cones and Coca-Cola like other kids did. So why were they all staring?

It had not occurred to me to retreat to the house, although now as an adult with many more battle scars from being eye-balled, the lure of the womb is much stronger. Besides, if I had gone inside, my mother would have given me a reassuring hug and sent me out again to face the world. She thought I could cope, so I did.

It took several days of participating in staring contests and answering piercing questions before the other kids got used to how I looked and invited me to play.

Kids: What's wrong with you? Why do you walk that way?

Me: I was born that way.

Kids: But why? Is it catching?

Me: I was in a hurry to be born, but the doctor wasn't ready, so the nurses tried to stop me and they hurt my brain, but they couldn't stop me, and here I am. And no, you can't catch it.

Kids: Oh, okay.

Some of those encounters seemed to last forever. I couldn't help wishing I were more like Sandy, who seemed to find her place right away, although later she confessed it was not that easy for her to make friends either. Lucky for me, I was a good hide-and-seek player—I could sniff out those playmates who were the hardest to find. Later on I became a dynamite punchball player, despite my discombobulated way of running around the bases. Sally, who lived across the street, did become one of my best friends, but it was the result of choice, not default. We spent many an afternoon playing on those backyard swings, guessing which peach from the nearby tree harbored a worm.

In my life since this trial at age five, I have engaged in many other struggles to enter new territories, to be born and reborn, not all with such successful outcomes. On more than one occasion, I have built womblike structures around me as protection against unwelcoming strangers who say it is not my time to emerge. But images of my insistence and persistence on the day of my birth, and of my mother's scratching and biting on my behalf, keep reappearing in my mind, and invariably a fist emerges from behind the womb opening, no matter how small.

3. Close Encounters with the Clueless

What's wrong with you?
You're so inspirational!
Were you born that way?
Are you sick? Is she sick?
Is she, you know, slow?
Or drunk? A bit too much chardonnay, perhaps?
You're so courageous.
If it were me, I'd never leave my house.
I'd wish I were dead.
If you could choose, would you be normal?
I mean, even though you do so well.
Do you live with your mother? Do you work? Can you have
  sex?
Have you ever had a boyfriend? Was he a cripple, too? Or a
  saint?
What a shame—such a pretty girl.
You're so brave.
Aren't things better now for the handicapped?

4. The Beggar and the Cripple

"Spare change?"

I don't usually give to beggars, but I found myself strangely drawn to this disheveled young woman as she walked back and forth, her hand outstretched, in front of the Japanese restaurant down the street from my house. Her coat was shabby, torn at the sleeves, and splotched with coffee stains. Her hands and face were caked with dirt, as though she hadn't washed in a week. Although I am usually obsessive about cleanliness and will change a blouse when the least spot appears, it was as though I could see myself in her, someplace deep beyond the surface of her dirty face. So I wanted to rescue her, as I have sometimes yearned to be rescued from desperate situations.

Beggars usually arouse my fury, not my empathy. I not only am suspicious of being ripped off by a con artist but hate when others evoke my guilt, the beggar's empty hand reminding me of my middle-class life of plenty. Also, growing up with a disability has made the prospect of becoming a beggar all too real. While consciously I despise stereotypes and, as an activist, demand equal rights for disabled and other oppressed people, my mind harbors childhood images that threaten to erupt and take hold, images of cripples as beggars from Hollywood movies and telethons. I hate beggars because they could be me, or I could be them, in my worst fantasies. My rational self knows that beggars are simply poor people trying to survive, an oppressed group themselves, but when I encounter a beggar, I'm rarely able to think rationally.

Yet there I was, rapidly approaching this beggar, rummaging through my purse until I found a dollar bill. Grabbing the bill in my fist, I thrust it in front of me. As I walked toward her, her eyes caught mine and then slid right over my outstretched arm and became focused on my uncoordinated walk. When I was nearly in front of her, she abruptly turned around and began walking away from me. "Perhaps she has to pee," I thought, fully convinced I was deceiving myself. Maybe I was misjudging her. Not every rejecting look need be related to my disability; I have been rejected for other reasons. And not every look at my body need be rejecting. Admittedly, daily encounters with disability prejudice foster a touch of paranoia. But the way she eyed my off-balanced walk smacked of discomfort, if not disgust. I quickened my pace to catch up with her, determined to give her my dollar. She crossed the street, and I followed suit. I was a quick walker when I wanted to be, disability or not, and I soon overtook her. I put the dollar in her hand, but she pushed it back at me, muttering, "No, thank you." "Here, take this," I persisted. But she persisted back with another "No, I don't want it" and then ran off.

I was too dumbfounded to follow her this time, my cheeks tingling with shame. "Who else but a cripple would be refused by a beggar?" I found myself thinking. No rational self present here, only misconceptions, misjudgments, and a refusal to be looked down on by a common beggar. Now standing in front of my favorite Mexican restaurant where I had been going for years, dollar bill in hand, I decided to stop in for a margarita, to give myself time to think or perhaps to stop my thinking. After a few sips, the shame subsided long enough for me to drift off into a daydream. I imagined the beggar woman sitting on the next bar stool.

Harilyn: My name is Harilyn; what's yours?

Anna: Anna. That was weird, you running after me out there. You run pretty fast for a, you know, cripple.

Harilyn: Yes, I'm fast even if I'm not that well coordinated. You were pretty weird yourself, running away when all I wanted to do was give you a dollar. I thought you needed money. I just wanted to help.

Anna: You looked like you needed more help that I did. I mean, my life is not as bad as you think.

Harilyn: Nor is mine. But don't you hate standing on that street corner, having to rely on people's sympathy to buy you a cup of coffee?

Anna: I've been in worse places. I used to be with this really abusive guy. He'd punch me around. That was hell. This is a lot better. No one punches me out on the

street. The crowd protects me. What about you? Don't
you hate being a cripple?

Harilyn: Not at all. There are worse things.

Anna: How'd you get that way? Were you in an accident
or something?

Harilyn: No. I was born that way. Not enough oxygen at
birth.

Anna: Oh, Jesus. It would have been better if you had
died.

Harilyn: Why? I have a pretty decent life. A good job,
friends, a nice boyfriend.

Anna: A boyfriend? Can you fuck—I mean, have sex?

Harilyn: Why not? There are lots of ways to fuck.

Anna: Tell me about it. I think I've tried them all.

Harilyn: So tell the truth. Why did you walk away when
I tried to give you the money?

Anna: It seemed cheap to take money from someone like
you, crippled and all. I would hate for people to see.
I mean, you need it more than I do.

Harilyn: No, I don't. And I really wanted you to have it.

Anna: Yeah, why'd you want to give it to me?

Harilyn: Because you really needed it.

Anna: Bullshit. Why'd you want to give it to me?

Harilyn: I guess it would make me feel good.

Anna: Well, it's not my job to make the cripples of the
earth feel good.

Harilyn: Don't you think you also make the noncripples
of the earth feel good by taking their money?

Anna: Nope. I play on their guilt.

Harilyn: You make me feel guilty, too.

Anna: Oh. How disgusting. To make a crippled person
feel guilty. Talk about guilt, mine. "There but for the
grace of God go I."

Harilyn: I feel the same way about you.

Anna: What? You couldn't possibly pity me. I'll get out of
my situation. You won't.

Harilyn: My situation is all right. I have a good life—
family, friends, love, sex, work, money, everything I need.

Anna: Really? Mine ain't too bad either, although I could use a few extra bucks.

Harilyn: Tell you what. I'll believe you if you believe me.

Anna: It's a deal. Now how about giving me that buck that you shoved in my face back there? Or better yet, since you're doing so good, make it five. And next time you see me, say something friendly instead of just waving your guilt money at me.

Harilyn: Right. We "guilt producers" have to stick together.

I awakened from my dreamy state to find the dollar bill still clutched in my hand. No Anna in the next seat. Just the bartender asking if I wanted another margarita. "No need," I explained, leaving the dollar as part of his tip.

5. The Stare

I feel her eyes before I see them in that coffee shop around the corner, my second home, with its gray-and-white Formica counter and rickety, red stools that have horsehair stuffing peeking out, scratching my thighs when I'm foolish enough to wear a short skirt.

Every morning, corn muffin and coffee. No need to order. George, the waiter, sees me meandering in and thrusts the muffin on the grill while he pours just the right amount of milk into my coffee cup, knowing my shaky hand, a badge of cerebral palsy, has a poor track record, as likely to douse the counter as the coffee.

I look up, my sense of comfort shattered by the face across the counter that wants me gone, her eyes glaring, filled with fury and disdain, watching my involuntary movements—my limbs and facial muscles dancing without my consent—imposing on them her own fears and fantasies.

Her lips contort in ways that mock mine, mumbling words of disgust to a nonexistent neighbor on the next stool. George, always the good observer, gets between us, coffeepot in hand, engaging her in idle conversation to give me a moment to remember who I am.

I overhear her longing to live in my area—Greenwich Village—and her conviction that she could never afford it, and I, a longtime resident, jump in, offering her guidance about how to look for cheap sublets, knowing she has little chance of success. Not in my neighborhood! The news that I am a native, with a rent-stabilized apartment no less, transforms me from freak to friend, not necessarily a gift as I become prisoner of her compensatory banter about her mother who had a stroke and who, she insists, shakes worse than I do. And isn't it amazing that I can do so well, living on my own in a neighborhood most people would die for? As the telethon talk continues, I debate whether my role as educator has to begin at breakfast when all I want to do is to enjoy the sweetness of my corn muffin and shoot the breeze with George.

6. Always the Other

"Is she sick? What's wrong with her? Does it hurt her? Can you keep her away?" he asked to no one in particular as we stepped into the elevator together. I had hoped he was referring to some weirdo in the hall, but as the elevator began descending, his voice began rising as he pointed at me and kept talking to someone else—perhaps to my companion, flummoxed into silence, or to some imaginary person he wished were there to protect him from the spectacle of me.

What's wrong with him that he would ask, "What's wrong with her?" To this bland-looking man, indistinguishable in his modest gray suit from the average guy yet defined by our culture as "retarded" (now called "intellectually disabled," a more accurate, less judgmental term), the boundaries between different and sick are blurry. Yet his reaction was not a reflection on him or the IQ number used to label him but rather a reminder to me for perhaps the millionth time that to most people, unfamiliar with my disabled countenance, I look different—no, weird—an object of pathos, pity, paternalism, prayer: "But for the grace of God . . ."

Not that the so-called normals, or Nobel Prize winners, for that matter, react to my disability any better. But they do know better than to say what they fear aloud—that is, usually they do, or maybe only sometimes. "What happened to you?" "Were you in an accident?" "Were you born that way?" "Too bad there's no cure." I ponder whether I would be any less hurt if a supposed intellectual rather than a man seen as intellectually wanting viewed me as an eyesore. I can more easily curse the smart-ass, yet I expect more from my fellow passenger and comrade who knows the pain of being labeled without being seen. But he did not see me.

"I'm disabled, not retarded." How often I've taken my seat at the table at this man's expense. So now I feel humiliated to be degraded by someone lower down in society's hierarchy of lives worth living. But his not knowing his place works to his

advantage. He voices his anxieties without social constraint, perhaps a lesson worth learning.

Is there no anonymity, no right to silence, even between floors?
Finally, my empathy with his anxiety wins out over my shame—
or is it my fury? "She's fine," I hear myself saying, startled by how
I've objectified myself. "What she has doesn't hurt." He's not convinced and races out the elevator door, first chance, still muttering
to himself.

Where is she, my friend, or should I say, my silent partner?
She recovers her speech through monologue. "He's retarded, you
know. Retarded people are very perceptive, just like children.
Once I was walking along the street after fighting with my boyfriend, and this retarded kid came up to me and asked why I was
angry. Wasn't that amazing?" I was amazed how alone I felt, my
only witness unsure of her alliances, when I needed her to acknowledge the assault even if the perpetrator could not be held
accountable.

"You are too sensitive," my mother always said. Perhaps she is
right. I'll never get over not being seen as all right.

7. Why I Am *Not* Inspirational

My feet are too large, for starters—size twelve, huge for a woman. I have to go to a special shoe store. Oops, there's another word—*special*—that makes you think I deserve the "inspirational" label.

Well, frankly, I'm not inspirational. I'm damn boring, if you ask me, which you rarely do. I worry about paying the rent, eating too much chocolate, and finding telltale wrinkles—sound inspirational yet?

I'm addicted to *Law and Order*, chardonnay with a nice bouquet, and—here's the biggest confession—McDonald's french fries. And yes, I talk with a disability accent that makes you wonder whether I've had too much of that chardonnay. My walk is less than graceful, not at all helped by those size twelves—I wish they were nines—but surely the *I* word requires more than that.

I know, I know, if you were me, you'd never leave your house and maybe even kill yourself. So I am inspirational because I haven't committed suicide—yet. I thought suicide was illegal—they arrest you for that, don't they? Although it would appear that those laws are changing, at least for the likes of me. "Assisted suicide"—that's what they call it. "Murder," "genocide"—that's what many of us with disabilities call it. Pressure to die to convenience others—people who can't imagine having a good life on a respirator or feeding tube (such lack of imagination), people who think such lives are too costly (is it better to invest dollars in wars and prisons?).

I'll tell you why I am inspirational: I put up with the barriers, the barricades, the bullshit you put between us to avoid confronting something—probably yourself—and still pay the rent on time and savor dark chocolate. Now that takes real courage.

But most of the time, I'm dull, doing my thing and dreaming of the day when all shoe stores carry size twelve.

8. Home

Home is being silent. It is not having to listen to anyone else, not having to make conversation and worry about whether others understand me, not having to consult with anyone about what to eat or drink or what to do next. It is refusing to answer the phone, drinking sweet cups of coffee, sitting in front of my living room window looking at magical tree trunks or naked neighbors. It is writing, painting, dreaming, musing, or becoming mindless. It is being by myself but not being lonely or anxious to start or stop. Home is me by myself without the impulse to flee. It is not being intruded on. It is relishing the moment without fearing the hour. It is writing this word without feeling pressured to start the next. It is hearing sounds and voices without scrutinizing what they mean. It is having all the time in the world to speak from a place in my belly that is usually silent. It is feeding my plants. It is listening to the birds out my window. Home is not threatening myself with humiliation and ruin. It is just being in the world without demand or expectation. It is hiding in a safe place.

II

On Leaving Home

9. Wedding Day, 1933

It was June 30, 1933, my mother's twenty-third birthday, and her boss, an attorney on Court Street in downtown Brooklyn who was famous for working his legal secretaries to death for little pay, gave her the afternoon off in a sudden moment of generosity. Her tall, dark, exotic-looking boyfriend waltzed by to spend a celebratory afternoon with her, having gone to his pattern maker's job at an ungodly hour to wangle an early departure from the clothing factory. As they left her office building, they glanced across the street to Brooklyn Borough Hall, then at one another in mutual consent, and spontaneously decided to get married, the fulfillment of four years of daily daydreams. My mother recruited a friendly-looking stranger off the street to be their witness in front of the court clerk, for neither of them dared to invite relatives or friends to observe the sinful act. Despite the lengthy courtship, they had not yet overcome the resistance of their two families, each of whom was totally convinced that the other was not really Jewish, and, of course, mixed marriages defied the Ten Commandments. My mother's family, the Rubinsteins, who were Ashkenazi Jews, could not make heads or tails of my father's family, the Roussos, who had an Italian-sounding name, spoke a weird language that sounded a lot like Spanish and not at all like Yiddish, and with their olive skin and dark features looked anything but Jewish. The Rousso clan claimed to be Sephardic Jews, but what in the world was that? No Jews Mama and Papa Rubinstein ever knew ate rice and beans on Friday night instead of matzo ball soup. The Rousso family disapproved of those fair-skinned outsiders who came from Russia instead of the little Sephardic town of Monastir in the old country (part of the Ottoman Empire, later Yugoslavia, now Macedonia); the Rubinsteins didn't know Ladino, the Sephardic language combining Spanish and Hebrew, and couldn't dance to Greek and Turkish music, so essential to the Sephardic tradition. Evelyn Rubinstein and David Rousso, my parents, who had been initially attracted to one another in part because of their differences, had not made much headway in resolving the cultural war between the clans. They figured it would be quite a while before their families would lay down their arms and approve of an official wedding, with a rabbi and everything. And here was the marriage license bureau right across the street. It was a sign.

After the clerk declared them husband and wife, Eve and Dave took to the subway to find an appropriate place to celebrate. A real, live opera in Manhattan seemed just the thing, although neither had ever before been to an opera. After buying the cheapest tickets, they found themselves sitting in the topmost balcony, listening to Bizet's *Carmen*. All they could see from where they sat snuggling was that the opera star playing Carmen was very, very fat. "Who in the world would want her?" they wondered, trying to follow the romantic plot line described in the libretto. And then they started laughing. And couldn't stop. Finally, the usher evicted them from the theater, which only made them laugh even harder.

What to do next after the eviction? "Why not visit our old haunts?" my mother, the social director of the duo, proposed. Much later on, after my mother was really my mother, she told me how she, her older sister Sarah, and her best friend, Sylvia, would hang around together like the Three Musketeers, and wherever they would go—to the local branch library or the park on the Lower East Side or Coney Island—my father would show up to flirt with my mother and accompany the trio. "I never knew how he knew where we would be, but he was always there," Mom explained. These were the days when young ladies could not go out unaccompanied with men, particularly men who were not approved of by their families. So Aunt Sarah and Sylvia would serve as chaperones, always promising that they would not tell Mama Rubinstein about the tall, dark stranger who was ever present in their midst, and my father would serve as the gallant protector of the fragile ladies, who were by no means fragile.

Now unencumbered by chaperones, Eve and Dave found their way to the green benches of the familiar grassy park on Houston Street and Avenue A near where my mother lived, sitting with their arms entwined, watching shouting schoolchildren being daredevils on swings, and imagining the voices of their own children. Then they continued their southward journey to the Fulton

Fish Market on the East River waterfront near the Manhattan side of the Brooklyn Bridge, where they followed their tradition of ordering from one of the outdoor stalls a single plate of the fish special of the day for twelve cents. He fed her and she fed him as they imagined the fried fish transformed into wedding cake.

As the daylight began vanishing, they meandered back uptown toward my mother's family's apartment, where my father would drop my mother off and hop the subway for the Rousso household in New Lots, Brooklyn. On the way, they passed the Sephardic social club on Delancey Street, where their romance had been born. It seemed like either yesterday or decades ago when Eve's friend Goldie had dragged her to a club that she had just discovered, populated by gorgeous dark-skinned men who looked nothing like Goldie's or Eve's brothers. Goldie had taken a shine to Dave and wanted to show him off to her dear friend. A fatal error. Dave could not take his eyes off my mother. "She looked so American, like she really belonged in this country, and she talked nonstop, so I didn't have to worry about what to say," my father would later explain to his children—me, Sandy, and Eli—who were then, as now, so captivated by his storybook tale. They had danced all night, leaving Goldie on the sidelines, seeing red. Goldie dropped out of the scene after that night, and my father began popping up, like a jack-in-the-box, wherever my mother turned.

Finally, after a slow-paced walk, the newlyweds wound up at the Rubinstein apartment door. No thought of sleeping together or even public smooching, lest my mother's older brother see them and run after my father, the "non-Jew," with a baseball bat. What were their parting words? I would get only silence in response to that question. Within minutes, my father was back on the train to Brooklyn, perhaps envisioning the real Jewish wedding with the Rubinstein apple strudel and the Rousso baklava that would have to wait for another day.

10. Dancing

I remember my mother leading the line dances at Sephardic family events. These were gatherings on my father's side of the family, Sephardic Jews who centuries ago had been expelled from Spain and had scattered throughout the Ottoman Empire, where they maintained their unique Sephardic traditions, including their language, Ladino, while adapting some of the Ottoman culture, such as Turkish food, music, and dance. My mother, an Ashkenazi Jew and hence not of their group, had nonetheless mastered many of their complicated, hybrid customs, including their style of dancing. Although she was heavy-set and had wide feet and unshapely legs with blue varicose veins, her physical reality didn't stop her from being graceful on the dance floor. Whenever she would hear Greek or Turkish music, the sounds of the bouzouki, clarinet, and lute, she would immediately find her way to the dance floor and join the line dance in progress. After decades of marriage to my father, she could dance effortlessly, with such precision that those on either side of her could follow in her footsteps when they lost their way. And so, without intent, she became the master teacher. Women struggling to learn the steps would grab my mother's arm, and she would patiently instruct, demonstrate, and literally put their bodies into place when all else failed. She was the "Yiddisha," as my father's mother fondly, or at times not so fondly, called this Yiddish-speaking Ashkenazi girl who had pushed her way into the pure-blood Sephardic family; yet she could dance to "Zorba the Greek" at least as well as Zorba.

But Zorba, a.k.a. my mother, had far less luck teaching me, her youngest child, to dance. Not that she didn't try to teach me, with determination and insistence that I could learn despite my poor coordination. And I did learn when I was five years old and uninhibited about my unseemly gait and body movements; at that age, I loved the freedom, the spirit of those line dances, and the sense of belonging they provided. But as I grew older, I internalized the stares of bewilderment and judgment that were so frequently directed at me by people in my world. I became ashamed of my body and, as a result, lost my capacity to get up on the dance floor in public, watching instead from the sidelines, the dance steps slowly fading from my memory. When my mother was successful in dragging me onto the dance floor, those few times when my longing overpowered my self-consciousness, I became the very klutz, or worse, pathetic freak that I had feared.

My mother and I now dance only in my head—in my mother's case because she has been dead and buried for many years, in my case because the voices of judgment continue to stop me dead in my tracks. Perhaps, though, it is not yet too late to "come out" as a dancer. Longing is a powerful motivator, and my shame about so much I had learned to dislike about myself has diminished with both age and my involvement in the disability rights movement. I have been inspired by the growing number of people with disabilities, including those with cerebral palsy, who have become professional dancers and have recast their unusual body movements as assets, not deficits, to the dance process. I suspect that one of these days when I hear the bouzouki, I'll think of my mother and say, "What the hell! If a 'Yiddisha' can do it, so can a gimp."

11. Exploding Beans

One pot turned into two, two into four. Yet still the beans were swelling and spilling over the top of the well-worn aluminum pots. I was wiping and sweating and praying, all at the same time. At age ten, I had been pressed into service to cook the Friday night beans. As usual, my mother had lost track of time while engaged in some good deed on behalf of the organization where she volunteered, only to suddenly look at her watch and realize that my dad would be coming home momentarily to a dinnerless and wifeless kitchen. He was a seemingly mild-mannered man but not in the face of certain injustices.

It had always been Sandy who got the last-minute call with instructions on how to throw the meal together. She was the older daughter and handier around the house. An obsessive student, I was considered the scholar of the family, which in my mind was a euphemism for being an undomesticated klutz. But tonight my sister herself was out meandering—boys had finally caught her eye at age fifteen—leaving me and our black cat, Desi, as my mother's only choices for potential cooks.

I realized that I was in trouble as the white, puffy great northern beans began spilling down the front of the stove onto the floor. My shrieks brought Desi running into the kitchen to see what was up. Fearful that he might burn his paws in the water that was rapidly spreading across the red-and-white-checkered linoleum tiles, I turned off all the stove burners, the first sane decision I had made thus far.

An expert in cleanup—my job around the house had always been to clean the dining table and wash the dishes—in relatively short order, I mopped up the floor and scraped most of the beans off the surface of the stove. Leaving the four pots with their now-dormant contents on the stove, I picked up Desi and sat with him on a kitchen chair awaiting judgment. I prayed that my mother would beat my father home so that I wouldn't have to explain both the white gunk in the pots on the stove and my mother's absence. Mercifully, it was my mother's key that I heard in the door first—I could always guess correctly by how each fiddled with the key. She also tended to hum no matter how late she arrived, a dead giveaway for eager ears. She entered, carefully balancing four brown paper bags filled with groceries, from which she was intending to whip together the nonbean portion of the meal. Once she put the grocery bags down on the counter, she eyeballed the four pots of semicooked beans on the stove and looked inquisitively toward me.

"They just started taking over and multiplying," I explained. "When I ran out of pots, I gave up."

"How many beans did you put in the first pot?" she inquired.

"Oh, the whole box," I responded. And my mother immediately began laughing.

"You were only supposed to use a cup. Beans expand. Don't you know that?"

"How was I supposed to know that?" I wondered silently, sure of my domestic incompetence. I was sufficiently relieved that she was laughing rather than screaming that I laughed, too. But I vowed to avoid further cooking adventures; clearly, my culinary arts gene was defective.

My mother discarded the beans and started from scratch, using a single cup of dried beans that grew into a quantity that, when combined with other foods, was enough to feed my family of five. Friday night beans was a delicious dish from my father's Sephardic tradition in which the beans were ultimately cooked in a tomato-like soup with flanken meat and bones. We ate it every Friday night of my childhood. Once my mother was successfully engaged, humming as she cooked, which was her usual way, I fled upstairs, pussycat in hand. I did my homework, where I knew I was a star, and Desi purred in my lap.

My mother got good mileage out of my beans story—everyone laughed when she recited it at family gatherings—but she never asked me to cook again. Although my mother was a good short-order cook, she didn't love to cook, so she made little deliberate attempt to pass the art on to me or my sister. She cooked because my father expected it, and she instructed my sister because my father insisted on eating, even when she was doing her charitable work around town. But given a choice, my mother would have made my father take her out to dinner every night, and she did when they got older. She had bigger plans for her daughters than cooking for demanding husbands. It didn't occur to her that the bean fiasco and her subsequent failure to enlist me on further cooking expeditions might have taken its toll on my image of myself as a real woman. Real women intuitively knew how to cook, or so I thought.

In the several years since my mother's death, my sister and I have sometimes scrambled around the kitchen, trying to recreate those Friday night meals, in part to recapture our mother. Or rather, Sandy cooks and I clean up while watching intently, hoping to master cooking. Not that I need to cook. Where I live, there are a million take-out places offering meals quicker and cheaper than starting from scratch. Yet still there is the longing, "If only I could." At one sister-to-sister encounter, Sandy decided to make beans. She resorted to a Sephardic cookbook.

"Don't you know how to make them?" I asked in surprise.

"No, Mom never really taught me," she explained. "Mom gave me blow-by-blow directions. I just followed, by rote. I didn't really learn. Or want to learn. I was so angry at her for putting the burden on me. You were so lucky. You got to study."

"I studied because I couldn't cook," I explained.

"You studied because you were smart. I wasn't smart."

Ah, the misconceptions we both held about ourselves. Turning the pages of the Sephardic cookbook in silence, we finally hit upon the bean recipe, replete with the note that the dish is best served on Friday night.

"Well, if I'm so smart and you're such a good cook, maybe we can throw together this bean dish," I suggested. "I know for sure we start with one cup of beans."

12. My Sister

When I was about nine or ten, my older sister, Sandy, told me the meaning of "fuck," which I had been using somewhat indiscriminately because I liked the sound of the word. I was appalled by her definition. "A boy puts his what into a girl's what?" I asked, turning red. She assured me I'd get used to the idea and someday actually like it. I thought she was putting me on.

She showed me how to put sanitary napkins into the belt the first time I bled and was doubled over with pain and embarrassment. Having already been menstruating for several years, she also gave me a Midol tablet for the pain and told me that getting my period was good news. She was lying, of course.

I asked about kissing after my first serious date when I was ancient, close to thirty, and too old to ask my friends who were doing a lot more than kissing. I didn't much like it and wondered if I was a weirdo. "You have to develop a taste for kissing, like olives. Just keep at it," Sandy said reassuringly. She was right this time.

The five-year age gap between us now seems insignificant. We talk, share secrets, support one another, and pal around like age compatriots—best friends, in fact. I feel lucky that we are so close, although I get peeved when people have the audacity to ask which of us is older. But when we were growing up, the age gap seemed huge. She was expected to keep her eye on me whether she wanted to or not, taking me along to the movies when she went with her friends, and even on some dates with her husband-to-be, although I was given strict instructions: "Forget everything you hear, and don't look when we neck." When we now reflect on her big sister/ second mother responsibilities then, she insists she didn't mind. But how could she not have? How could she find and define herself apart from the family when she was stuck dragging her kid sister around—and a kid sister with a disability, no less, whose weird way of walking and talking must have been a source of embarrassment? I, in turn, was expected to listen to her, which I suppose I did, since I was a pretty compliant kid. I also looked up to her since she had all the skills I seemed to lack. She was amazingly artistic, made friends easily, was physically nimble, and, with her nondisabled, curvaceous body, was able to attract lots of boys, at times to my father's chagrin. However, I considered myself a better student, a message that my mother reinforced, perhaps as compensation for my physical limitations. My mother would brag to relatives about my reading scores and grades, noting how I was surpassing my older sister. Her bragging made me proud but also uneasy; I knew too well the pain of being put down. Fortunately, Sandy never appeared to hate me for my mother's comments, although like all good older sisters, she tormented me from time to time: "How can you wear a striped blouse with a plaid skirt? What's wrong with you?" "You know you need a bra. Your boobs are bobbing." I suppose I should have taken the latter as a compliment, given how flat-chested I was, but I didn't.

Because Sandy came of age in the conservative, Cold War, a-woman's-place-is-in-the-home 1950s and I in the progressive, civil rights, women's rights, anti–Vietnam War 1960s, the five years between us amounted to a generation gap. Like many women of her generation, her primary goals were to marry and have children, and her first commitment has been to family, broadly defined—her children, her grandchildren, our parents, her parents-in-law, and various other family members, including, luckily, me. When I need help with anything, she is there. But as a result of her strong family focus, her work history has been spotty despite her two master's degrees, in teaching and art therapy, and her many talents. Over the past decade or two, we have had repeated conversations about her desire to work, but she has never seriously proceeded with job hunting.

In addition to family, Sandy's other major commitment has been to painting. Drawing on her talent and love of art, she has taken decades of classes and makes impressive paintings. But she has never viewed her art as "real work"; in that respect, her attitude mirrors society's disregard for artistic endeavors, especially when they do not translate into dollars. Her priorities are clear: She will skip painting classes to babysit a grandchild, take an aging relative to the doctor, or even be a shopping companion to her needy sister (me).

I, on the other hand, have always been more committed to school and career. The prevalence of disability stereotypes when I was growing up convinced me that I would never find a partner or have children, so achievement in the classroom and the workplace became central to my identity. While my focus on work at times made me doubt my womanhood—"real" women marry—this view was transformed to some degree by my involvement in the women's movement, which encouraged women to assume roles and sources of identity beyond the home. Not that family is unimportant to me, but it has never been primary.

I set my priorities early. I distinctly remember an incident that occurred during my junior high school years, when the basement of our house in Queens had flooded and my mother was desperately removing the water with buckets. I had just come home from school, when I heard her shouting up to me from the basement to come help her. When I got downstairs, she was knee deep in water, the bottom half of her housedress totally soaked. She instructed me to take off my shoes and socks, roll up my skirt, and grab a bucket. I hesitated and then did what she said, but only for about five minutes. At that point I told her I had to go to my room because I had a lot of homework to do and an algebra test the next day. Anger and disbelief spread over her face, but she didn't say a word—speechless, an unusual state for my mother. Had she yelled, I might have stayed at least a bit longer. Directly confronting her anger was at least as scary as failing a test. But I left, shoes and socks in hand, with some sense of guilt but not enough to stop me. My mother emerged, quite wet and bedraggled, some three hours later. She never said a word to me about the incident, although I did overhear her complaining to our next-door neighbor. "That daughter of mine left me stranded in the midst of that flood to do her homework. Can you imagine that? The nerve of that kid!" By the time of this flood, Sandy was already married and out of the house. Had she still lived at home, undoubtedly she would have helped my mother until the basement was dry.

Our difference in priorities has made Sandy and me ever so slightly incomprehensible to each another. I have difficulty understanding why she would forgo a painting workshop to go to the bar mitzvah of some distant relative, and she cannot understand why I won't put aside a writing project to attend a family gathering that, in her mind, is quite important. Sometimes we'll argue rather fiercely about these differences. I suppose it speaks to my high level of trust with her that she is one of the few people in the universe that I can talk back to and get angry at without fearing abandonment. Well, that's not quite true. I do fear that she'll never talk to me again, but she always does, no apologies needed. In fact, she usually acts as though my fits of anger never occurred. That's not necessarily good news, but her overlooking my anger is a lot better than my losing her. As different as we are, Sandy is a major, if not *the* major, source of support, stability, and sanity in my life. She keeps me connected to family, at times in spite of myself. I sometimes teasingly call her "Mother Earth," and who doesn't still need a mother? Besides, she taught me the meaning of "fuck," and there is nothing more basic than that.

13. Adolescent Conversation

Why didn't I talk about my disability with my best friends during adolescence? Why didn't it occur to me? My best friends—and everyone else—knew I had a disability. They accommodated my disability-related needs, pouring my soda so I wouldn't spill it, lending a hand when I tripped over my feet and fell. But there was never an open discussion. Perhaps to talk openly about it would have confirmed my difference at a time when I was so eager to be like everyone else. To me, my disability was not only a difference; it was also a defect. Why would I want to call attention to that? Perhaps I didn't have the words to speak about my disability; I never had discussed it with anyone and barely acknowledged it to myself. What would I have said? I can only imagine.

> Harilyn: Elaine, you are my best friend. I want to talk to you about something private.
>
> Elaine: Are you pregnant?
>
> Harilyn: No, I'm being serious.
>
> Elaine: I know what it is. I've been waiting for years. It's your handicap, right?
>
> Harilyn: I'm not really handicapped, but you know I have this thing called cerebral palsy. I'm lucky—it's a really mild case. You know, I can do everything.
>
> Elaine: Can you have sex?
>
> Harilyn: *What?*
>
> Elaine: Well, I'm curious. I wonder if I can have sex, and I don't even have a handicap.
>
> Harilyn: It's not a handicap, but yeah, I think I can.
>
> Elaine: You think you can, but you're not sure? Why don't you ask someone—like your doctor or your mother?
>
> Harilyn: I'd be too embarrassed. Anyhow, who would want to have sex with me?

Elaine: Lots of people. At least you're not tall and big boned like me. And you're nice looking.

Harilyn: I'd be too scared.

Elaine: You'd get over it. I did.

Harilyn: You've had sex?

Elaine: Almost. With a guy I like a lot.

Harilyn: I didn't know you were going out.

Elaine: I was afraid to hurt your feelings. You never even seemed interested in going out.

Harilyn: I wouldn't know what to do with a boy, even if someone asked me out, which no one would.

Elaine: No one will ask you unless you seem interested. You're too serious—stuck in your books. You need to think about dating and stuff. But first you should find out what you can do, you know, with sex. Maybe you could get a book from the library. I'd go with you if you want.

Harilyn: You would? Well, maybe. I'll think about it.

Elaine: So what exactly about cerebral palsy did you want to talk about?

Harilyn: I think I just wanted to say the words to you. It's felt like this secret I've had for a long time.

Elaine: Not much of a secret. Everyone knows. We can all see you have it.

Harilyn: And what does everyone think when they see I have it?

Elaine: It depends. People who don't know you very well feel sorry for you.

Harilyn: That's what I hate.

Elaine: But you didn't let me finish. Those of us who are your friends don't think much about it. We think you're pretty and very smart—you'll go to some Ivy League college for sure. But we are curious about your handicap or whatever you call it and never feel like we can ask you anything. You give off these vibes—like barbed wire—"Don't ask me or else!"

Harilyn: I just wish people wouldn't notice.

Elaine: But they do notice, so it would be better if you stopped pretending and talked about it.

Harilyn: You mean like, "Hello. I'm Harilyn Rousso, and I have cerebral palsy, and I can have sex—I think."

Elaine: Well, there's a start. Seriously, you need show other kids that you are okay with having this handicap and willing to talk about it.

Harilyn: So what would you say if I asked you why you are so tall and fat?

Elaine: I'd say it's partly genetic. And partly my metabolism—it's very slow, so I gain weight easily.

Harilyn: You didn't mind me calling you fat?

Elaine: Well, I didn't love it, but by answering you, I set you straight about why I'm so big. And I showed you that I'm okay with being the way I am.

Harilyn: I don't know if I'm as okay with having CP as you are with being tall and fat.

Elaine: Why not? Your handicap becomes a much bigger deal if you clam up about it.

Harilyn: I hate when strangers stop me in the street with stupid questions or comments about the CP. I want to run away.

Elaine: It's terrible! I've seen people do that lots of times, when we've been together. I feel like smacking them. Maybe if you felt okay talking with your friends about your handicap, you could talk back to those strangers who make stupid comments. Because your CP would no longer be a scary topic you can't talk about.

Harilyn: I think I'd have an easier time answering a stranger's question about my boobs than about my CP.

Elaine: Oh really? So why do you have such small boobs?

Harilyn: Oh, shut up! It's genetic, by the way.

14. On Leaving Home

When my mother told me in no uncertain terms that I had to go to college out of town, I thought she was joking. No, let's be honest—I was terrified. I was the kid who at age thirteen had insisted on being taken home from sleep-away camp after just one week because I was hysterically homesick. At age sixteen, I couldn't even stay at my favorite aunt's house for a weekend—I was crying so hard that she started to cry, too, and took me home by subway after just one night away; my aunt lived only ten miles from my parents' house.

My mother was dismayed by these failures. Her goal in life was to make me independent. From the physical side of things, she had done a spectacular job. She would never let my less-than-perfectly coordinated body stop me from doing anything. She encouraged me to climb steps, no matter how steep, to master a two-wheeled bicycle, no matter how poor my balance. She even taught me how to light matches when I expressed a desire to learn (probably so I could smoke cigarettes with my prepubescent friends); she had me light match after match until I conquered my fear of burning down the house. She never shared my fear of failure, totally convinced I could do everything and anything I wanted.

Going away to college is a transition point for many young people (at least for those who can afford to go away)—a major step away from family toward the world at large, the world of adulthood. For young people with disabilities, the typical challenges of leaving home are often complicated by their reliance on family members to help them perform tasks of daily living like bathing or dressing. Yet well before the time most kids go off to college, I had mastered virtually every task of self-care and independent living that I would need to live away from home—except the confidence to go off and leave my mother behind. I felt too vulnerable.

My vulnerability partly resulted from the fact that I hadn't yet figured out how to make sense of my disability. I was too invested in an image of myself as "normal" to acknowledge a difference of any kind. Growing up, I had interpreted people's stares and taunts to mean that there was something wrong with me not only physically but also globally. I felt that I was less than human, some kind of freak. I feared that to acknowledge my disability was to accept the freak status that others imposed on me—and that I, in my darkest moments, imposed on myself. I would much later discover to my astonishment and relief that many other people with disabilities had refused to see themselves as disabled for reasons similar to mine, but during my youth, I was quite alone with my confusion, since I knew no one else who had a disability. My mother was little help here. Her response to my pain at the staring, questions, and nasty comments from the outside world was that I should change the way I walk and move my body so I would look more "normal." I don't think she saw me as less than human or freakish, but she did hold the typical views of that time that a disability was a defect to be fixed, normalized. I misconstrued her efforts to minimize my disability-related characteristics as confirmation that there was a freakish creature living within me that needed to be contained and tamed.

Regrettably, my mother and I never had open conversations about my disability. It was one of those taboo topics that emerged only sporadically, usually in a crisis, when someone had said something particularly hurtful to me or when my mother was trying to coax me to practice looking "normal." I would react with refusal and denial, and she, in turn, would back off. Aside from my mother, none of my family members even mentioned my disability, although they assisted me when I needed help. No doubt they picked up on my resistance to talking about the topic. Unintentionally, the family conspiracy of silence confirmed my worst fears about what my disability meant. In my mind, something that couldn't be spoken about had to be really bad.

Part of what enabled me to maintain my stance of denial, at least with people who knew me, was that I was smart. I was a very successful student; people overlook a lot when you do well academically. Also, I had a pretty face and a good figure; I may have moved in odd ways, but, by some standards, I was considered attractive—or at least not a total turnoff.

I was afraid that if I left home to go to college, I would be faced with endless stares from people who didn't know me, with no one there to defend me. At least at home, I had a protector, my mother. If I couldn't do things one way, she would figure out another. If someone tried to stop me from doing something or to deny me an opportunity, she would take the person on and win. While her responses to the teasing and staring were far from perfect, at least she was there to hear my pain and brush away my tears. It was only with her that I would talk about my horrific encounters. I couldn't imagine fending off all by myself the stares, the questions, and the emotional distress they caused.

Another reason that going away to college seemed so impossible was that in my mind, my academic achievement was very much connected with my mother's presence. My mother had been a frustrated academic. Although she was an excellent student in high school, her parents had forbidden her to go on to college, despite prodding from her teachers, because they needed her to work to help support their large family. My mother received a commercial diploma from high school, substituting stenography, typing, and bookkeeping for her coveted academic subjects. After graduation, she spent her work life first as a secretary for a pair of lawyers and then as a Jane-of-all-trades for my father, who had started a women's clothing company in the garment district.

My mother had never had the opportunity to pursue her own intellectual interests. Thus, when I asked for her assistance—mainly to do term papers, which often seemed like overwhelming tasks requiring extensive research with tight deadlines—she eagerly agreed. We were a great team. Sitting together at the kitchen table with a few dozen open books around us, she typed and threw out ideas while I dictated to her my own thoughts and expanded on her suggestions, the hours passing well into the night. We got lots of A's. But I also developed the conviction that I couldn't do it without her. In addition, many of the papers we did together were in the field of literature—analyses of fiction, plays, poetry that were "required reading" for high school. Although I loved to read, writing about literature proved particularly problematic for me. My self-doubts about my normalcy and humanity had translated into a fear that I wasn't quite human enough to understand what the writers and/or the characters were experiencing, so I needed the input of my quite empathetic and, in my mind, totally normal mother to get the analyses right. Thus, academic achievement overall helped me cover up my disability and the feelings of abnormality that went along with it, but some types of academic work actually reinforced those feelings. My mother's presence, once again, was a counterbalance, ensuring that my presumed defects would not be revealed.

While my mother was willing to help me with term papers and so many other aspects of my adolescent life, she knew that I needed to learn how to separate and survive without her. She may have wanted more freedom herself, for at times my demands and neediness were burdensome. She assumed, perhaps rightly, that I could not separate in her presence. Sending me to college out of town at a time when many of my friends were doing the same must have seemed like the ideal solution.

I applied to three colleges in Massachusetts—Wellesley, Smith, and Brandeis—as well as Queens College, a local, publicly funded college that I was sure to get into, although in my mother's mind it was not really an option. "Over my dead body," she insisted. My first choice was Wellesley, because I was an academic snob and at that time, it was the most prestigious and had the highest admission standards of the three schools. My sense of self-worth went down a notch when I received the rejection letter, but that disappointment was countered by my acceptance at both Smith and Brandeis. I ultimately chose Brandeis, partly on the basis of my awareness that my father was very impressed with this prominent university founded with the support of the Jewish community, and I was eager to please him. Also, unlike Smith, Brandeis was co-ed, and because I was uneasy around boys, fearful of their rejection as potential romantic and sexual partners, I knew that running away to a girls' college would only reinforce my problem. I suppose even in those days I did have a modicum of mental health.

For a couple of months, I basked in the glow of having been accepted by two prestigious colleges. For a while I was able to push aside my fears of leaving home—and, most important, my mother. The fears began to reappear when, about a month before

I was to leave for college, my mother and I attended a gathering for incoming Brandeis freshmen who lived in the New York City area. Nothing horrendous happened, except that I found myself surrounded by a large group of people whom I didn't know, and although everyone was cordial, as the only person with a visible disability, I felt immediately uneasy and fearful of rejection. Although my mother was right by my side most of the time, her presence was not that comforting. I cried when we left the event, and even though my mother was sympathetic, she didn't quite grasp my impending sense of doom. I would be going off to college where I would be left in the company of polite but uncaring strangers who would see me as different and defective, reinforcing my own self-doubts, with no one to calm my fears.

I have a vivid memory of the day my parents packed the car with all my paraphernalia and drove me off to college. Lula, the woman who had been cleaning our house for close to a decade, said without malice but with direct knowledge of my past separation failures, "I know you'll be back home in a few weeks. You'll never stay." Caught up in the frenzy of leaving, I was too emotionally numb to respond to her comment, but I suspect that I both feared and hoped she was right.

The drive to college was uneventful; my numbness kept me calm. When we arrived, we drove to my dorm to unload my stuff. While most freshmen had roommates, I had been assigned a single room even though I had not requested it. Perhaps the housing office assumed cripples were not companionable. But I was glad. Given my self-consciousness about my disability, I couldn't imagine sharing a room with a stranger. I would quickly discover that at least for the first few weeks of college, having a roommate would have been advantageous. At least I would have had someone to eat meals with in the dining hall. But for the moment I was relieved to have a private space in which to hide.

When my parents left, I don't think I cried or made a scene, which would have been too humiliating. I tended to have a delayed reaction to crises in any case. Also, freshmen were required to attend a series of orientation sessions the very afternoon of our arrival, so I had reasons to keep moving without thinking or feeling. That first night, at an orientation banquet, I met a first-year graduate student in math, a very friendly, handsome young man who hung out with me for much of the evening. Given my date-less history and my fears of rejection, I was shocked by what appeared to be his interest in me. I found myself fantasizing that college was the beginning of a new life for me where I would have boyfriends like other girls and be "normal." It was like waking up to a new world that I had wanted all my life but had never thought possible. That fantasy never became a reality, at least not then. I never saw that graduate student after that evening.

The next morning, when the reality of my abandonment hit me, despair and loneliness overwhelmed me. They would remain my constant companions for the next few months, with periodic reappearances until I graduated from Brandeis. The first few weeks were the worst; every day I went through the same cycle of emotions. I felt most despondent when I woke up and could not imagine getting through the day. But my compulsion to achieve academically, or at least not to humiliate myself by failing out, propelled me out of bed and into the shower. After dressing, I dragged myself to the dining room for breakfast, inevitably alone, wondering how I was going to manage my tray of food, especially the liquids like coffee or milk, without making a spectacle of myself. In those days I would never have been willing to bring attention to my disability by asking for help. I would gobble down my food, which was comforting but not terribly appealing, worry about how others perceived me as I sat by myself at a long, often empty table, and try not to look too miserable. Later I would learn tricks to cover up my isolation and misery, like choosing a table where other students were sitting, even if they never said a word to me, and bringing a book so that I looked busy. After breakfast I would go to classes or to the library and get engaged in school-work, which distracted me from my unhappiness. My classmates were basically friendly, offering an initial smile, or at least not a judgmental stare, and my professors tended to be reasonable, civil, and, on occasion, kind, so sitting with them in an academic setting, even before I began to establish friendships, made me feel less alone. By evening I felt okay, telling myself that I could do this; I could survive. The absence of despair almost elated me. But by morning, the despair returned, and I'd have to work myself through the day again. Weekends were the worst. Without the structure of classes the desolation rarely left me.

The existence of cell phones might have saved me—or reinforced my dependency. As it was, I shudder to think how many hysterical collect calls I made to my parents that first semester from the pay phone down the hall from my dorm room, threatening, no, begging to come home, despairing about how I would survive, expressing fears of failing out. And my parents were not the only victims of my hysteria. I called every family member willing to accept a collect call—and I had a big family. My mother, hearing my distress (and perhaps feeling guilty for sending me away), sent me many funny cards and endless care packages. My father would write me a letter every Thursday filled with mundane details about life at home and fifteen dollars in cash, which in those days could buy most necessities with enough left over for a few pleasures, like chocolate. I fell apart when in one letter he described how he missed our regular school-day ritual of his squeezing fresh grapefruit juice for me and leaving me a nickel for the bus. It never occurred to me that he might miss me.

This family contact helped some, as did my beginning to make friends, mainly two or three girls who lived on my floor in the dorm; late in the night we would share the contents of one another's care packages from home and bemoan how much reading we had to get done by the next day.

I was also relieved to discover that I could do okay in most classes. Fortunately, few of my classes required papers. In the one course where I did have to write a paper without a chance to consult my mother, I got a C+, the lowest grade I would ever get, but I performed poorly partly because I didn't understand what the professor wanted. The paper required an analysis of a section of *The Iliad*, and in hindsight, I don't think my mother would have had the skills to help me.

Despite some beginning friendships and decent-enough grades during those initial months, I still was miserable much of the time and maintained the fantasy of going home. All that changed as the result of a conversation I had with my father a week or two before Thanksgiving. He said that if I didn't think I could make it at Brandeis, I could come home and he'd find me a job in his clothing factory. That was an unwittingly smart move on his part. The prospect of my coming home in defeat and working in what would be at best a low-level clerical position in his factory sounded so dreary that I couldn't bear it. I knew it would make me feel more freakish than ever. By the end of that conversation, I made up my mind that I had to stay at Brandeis and that I had to stop crying. For the next several years, well beyond my time in college, I did not allow myself to shed a tear or even to feel sadness for any reason. My endless crying and despair had become another source of difference, further evidence of defect, and I had to keep it under wraps. It was not until almost a decade later, when I started psychotherapy, that I allowed myself to cry again.

Once resigned to staying, I began to engage more fully with courses and friends and to disengage from my mother; the separation process was finally on track, albeit slowly. Although I had initially intended to major in math, one of my best subjects in high school, three days in an introductory calculus class for "advanced" students convinced me that I would never pass, much less succeed, in that subject. So I switched my major to economics, which was math related but more comprehensible and, thank goodness, required no term papers. The Economics Department proved to be a good home for me. It was small, and many of the faculty were young, enthusiastic, and eager to build their department by enticing more students to become economics majors. I became one of a handful of majors and, among the majors, one of the few women. After a somewhat mediocre first semester, I seemed to "get" economics, the kind of thinking and analysis behind it. I began to do exceedingly well in my courses and won considerable recognition and respect from my professors. While I still felt different, now my difference was based on my major, my gender, and my success rather than my disability, sources of admiration rather than disgust. Perhaps most important, through my study of economics, much of which focused on analyzing problems related to real people's needs, I began to get in touch with my own desire to help others who were deemed different and/or disadvantaged. Although at that time I did not yet see myself as fitting into that disadvantaged category—my focus was on people disadvantaged by poverty—my desire to use what I was learning to fight economic injustice and "save the world" was in part fueled by the injustices that I had encountered and the unacknowledged desire to save myself.

As a man involved in the business world, my father was thrilled by my choice of major. My mother, who had never taken an economics class and had no understanding of what majoring in economics meant, could make no sense of the textbooks I showed her and declared me "the smart one," much smarter than she was. While part of me knew she was could have mastered economics had she put her mind to it, I was relieved by the distance from her that my choice of major seemed to create. In some of my other subjects, I continued for a while to rely on her for advice, if not overt help, on writing term papers. Gradually, it became clear that my increasingly advanced subjects were beyond her scope of knowledge, and I discovered to my amazement that I could write successful papers by myself.

My fear of being seen as drastically different and hence os-tracized by everyone on campus did not come to pass. Initially, I did encounter stares from some students, but as people got to know me, their awareness of my disability seemed more or less to disappear. And, of course, I was lucky to be attending college in the 1960s, a time when being seen as different had begun to be-come an asset rather than a liability. My unusual walk and body movements were seen as one more idiosyncrasy among a growing group of idiosyncratic students. I made a few close friends and eventually came to feel that I belonged. One friendship became particularly important, with Ellen, who eventually became my roommate. A year behind me, she was exceptionally warm and sensitive, and we gravitated toward each other. In an unexpected way, she helped me separate further from my mother. The child of Holocaust survivors, she fell in love with a non-Jewish foreign student. Her parents were hell-bent on breaking up their rela-tionship, and during the year we lived together, there were many screaming phone calls between Ellen and her parents, which left her devastated. My mother loved Ellen and liked her boyfriend, but she was fearful that the conflict between Ellen and her parents would cause me stress, so she encouraged me to distance myself from her. I refused to comply and came to the realization, rather belatedly for an almost twenty-one-year-old, that my mother and I had different values and I could no longer rely on her ideals to guide me. It was both a sad and invigorating awakening of my mother's changing role in my life.

Through my friendships, my academic success, and my budding although vague sense of a "calling" to "save the world," I survived the four years and graduated with honors, although not without periodic lapses into panic and despair. But even in my most despairing moments, I no longer viewed going home to my mother as the solution. She remained a source of comfort but not a place to hide. Adulthood was upon me.

After graduation I never again lived at home, which upset my mother. She had thought that after I successfully separated to go to college, I would be able to resume living at home, albeit in a different way, but I knew I never could. For the first few years after college, I deliberately chose to live in different cities from my parents so there would be no chance of rekindling my dependency on my mother. When four years later I returned to New York City to go to graduate school in social work, I felt less endangered. By then I knew I could find my way in the world and handle my own fears of freakishness without her. Also, by this time I had decided to "save the world" by becoming a social worker, a role in which I would be working directly with people, rather than an economist, a less "hands-on" occupation, an indication that I was feeling much less freakish and much more like everyone else. One important factor that contributed to this transformation was my involvement in a women's consciousness-raising group a year or two after I graduated from college, where I discovered that many nondisabled women also felt defective as a result of their daily encounters with sexism. Thus, I was feeling much more connected to the community of women, although I had not yet begun to address my identity as a woman with a disability or to consider how disability bias compounds sexism. In any case, I no longer needed my mother to shield me from the judgments of others or myself.

Nonetheless, on my return to the city where my parents resided, I decided to get my own apartment, and my mother didn't protest; she even helped me find a place. By then I couldn't imagine living at home, and perhaps she couldn't imagine it either. We had separated irreparably, except for clothes shopping—she was still the best shopping companion I ever had—and periodic Friday night dinners, when she and my dad would take me out for wonderful dinners at fancy restaurants that I could never afford as a social worker.

My mother was right to insist on my separating from her. It was essential to my development as an independent woman. So many young women with disabilities have the opposite problem: mothers who won't let go, believing that they are their daughter's best caregivers and their most reliable protectors in an unsafe world. Some young men with disabilities have similar problems, although the societal views of men as more competent and self-sufficient than women often help sons with disabilities break the ties. I am grateful to my mother for her progressive attitude. It's not clear whether shipping me off to Brandeis, when I was feeling so emotionally vulnerable, was the best way to foster my separation; however, given the time period in which I grew up, maybe it was the only way. Among my generation, conversations between parents and children with disabilities about the impact of disability on their lives were rare. Many of my disabled friends described growing up in the same conspiracy of silence that I did. And having parents discuss disability as a source of prejudice and discrimination, as a civil rights issue rather than a medical issue, was unheard of then. My mother, in her defense, said she did try to talk to me about my disability, but I couldn't stand to listen; I would start to cry, so she would stop the conversation. I believe her. Hearing her talk about my disability probably felt like a confirmation of my difference, my freakishness, although maybe she started those conversations too late, when freak and disabled were already too entwined in my mind. Also, given her desire to normalize me, the words she chose may not have been the words I could hear.

She probably did the best she could. Yet I have paid a price for the abrupt breach in our relationship. I became and remain phobic about dependency. I have learned to associate dependency with becoming desperately, hopelessly needy, unable to function without the presence of that other person. Our culture, with its focus on independence, only reinforces that view. My reluctance to depend on others has been costly for me as a disabled and now aging woman who tends to refuse help because of its association with dependency—and for me as a partner and lover, who tends to resist the pleasures of dependency that are part and parcel of intimacy.

Yet I am hopeful about my ability to rethink dependency. Part of what has enabled me to untangle the reality of being disabled from my fear of being a freak was meeting many wonderful, beautiful, attractive, sexy, brilliant, outrageous, rebellious, revolutionary people with disabilities in the disability rights movement who were definitely *not* freaks—except when they chose to reclaim the word *freak* as their own and, as some have put it, "let their freak flag fly." They have shown me a way to be disabled and "normal," if I am foolish enough to set my sights so low. These same disabled folks have developed a take on dependency that I hope one day to emulate. They assure me that I can be both dependent and independent at the same time, that I can depend on others to meet my disability, aging, or just plain human needs and still maintain my independence by directing my own care. I can say with a sense of entitlement, "Please pour my chardonnay, but only to the half glass mark; throw in some ice so I'll be less likely to create a mess when I lift the glass to drink; and carry my glass over to that table where that handsome stranger is sitting." My disabled pals also claim I can lose myself in intimacy and still keep myself. I haven't accepted these assurances just yet. But who knows? Once I would never have believed I'd be able to leave my mother to go away to college.

15. Hideous Shoes

Hideous shoes: black, with laces, high on the ankle like my grandmother wore in the old country—my mother's last gift as I head for college, made special to support my crooked feet, she claims, but I suspect it's my virginity she's out to preserve.

The shoes take up permanent residence in the back of my dorm wardrobe, far from the sandals that prove more useful and the condoms that signify high hopes.

16. Driving High

When, in my early twenties, my mother announced that she was giving me driving lessons, our family doctor did not approve. He said he'd be afraid to be on the road with me, given my disability. "So take the train," my mother suggested.

I, too, had doubts about my driving, but these had little to do with my physical limitations. The image of myself as a driver was incongruous with some internal experience I had of myself of needing to be cared for and directed, of not being able to be in the driver's seat of my own life. There was something comforting and familiar about being driven around, of being picked up and delivered. Some of my fondest childhood memories were adventures in which my mother was behind the wheel, taking me shopping in some exotic store or to an out-of-the-way restaurant. My preference for passenger status held fast, even though I was otherwise radically independent, stubbornly making my own life decisions regardless of what anyone thought.

My mother recognized this incongruity or lapse in my independent self and sought to remedy it by insisting that I become a driver. Although it would take her several years of coaxing to overcome my resistance, she was persistent. She understood the dangerous consequences of surrendering to the impulse to let others take charge. My mother was strong and feisty and in many ways epitomized the independent woman. But when it came to major family decisions, she often succumbed to being submissive and a "good girl." My dad ruled. This was partly how she came to find herself living in unfamiliar territory, far from friends and family, in Queens, New York. In this situation, learning how to drive, largely without the help or blessing of my father, became her salvation.

I remember my mother's stories of how she conquered the gray 1951 Oldsmobile in our driveway. After my father went to work and we went to school, she would slowly back the car out, careful to avoid decapitating the red and yellow tulips around the edges of the lawn, and then practice right, left, and U-turns in the tree-lined neighborhood streets now devoid of schoolchildren. As she described it, parallel parking was the trickiest to master without the help of an experienced pair of eyes to guide her. But she would pick her victims carefully—already bruised cars that wouldn't mind another notch on their fenders, should she miscalculate, as she maneuvered to park behind them.

Our neighbors were far from pleased. "I'll call the police if you don't stop driving without a license," the woman living next door yelled. "Mind your own business, or I'll report your son for playing hooky," was my mother's immediate response. For her, taking on the police force seemed less daunting than being imprisoned in our less-than-stimulating neighborhood. She secured her license only after repeated tries. Then the world was hers. "Have you heard from Mom?" became my father's most frequently asked question, as he waited for her to show up, hours behind schedule, to cook his dinner and behave like his wife.

After learning to drive, my mother was eager to teach others in need of liberation; I was her most resistant pupil. I finally succumbed to her wishes when faced with the challenge of renting a car in the British Isles during an upcoming vacation with a childhood friend. By then I was in my late twenties and living in my own place in Manhattan; my parents had left Queens for a new house in Long Island. It was a grandiose idea to think that I could drive on the left side of the road when I had not yet mastered the right. But I was still young and eager to please my license-lacking traveling companion who had lived in Scotland and promised to show all, *if* I could do the driving. My mother seized her moment and showed up on my doorstep two or three times a week for almost two months to give me driving practice. I remember almost smacking a bus once and going the wrong way down a one-way street, but none of my misjudgments seemed to faze my mother. She showed fearlessness and perfect confidence that I could do this, I would do this, and I would like it. The promise of a delicious steak dinner at the end of each session and her unshakable will got me through those initial near disasters.

As skill replaced images of myself lying dead on the highway, I was surprised to discover an amazing sense of mastery and freedom emerging. I could drive myself anywhere in the world, not dependent on anyone else's desires or whims! My fantasies started nationally as I imagined driving to New Mexico to eyeball the magnificent red, orange, and purple sunsets while pretending to be Georgia O'Keeffe or journeying to Cape Cod off season to talk with the ocean and walk naked on the beach. Then I became more expansive, driving to kiss the Blarney stone. I also imagined speeding past our family doctor and giving him the finger. As I shared with my mother, tentatively at first, my newfound sense of freedom and began reeling off all the adventures I might undertake, she shrieked with pleasure and said, "Let's go." Her enormous enthusiasm surprised me. I suppose I had feared abandonment—that should I, her youngest child, become truly independent, she would become distant and disapproving. But clearly, she would not let me go so easily.

When I got my license on the first try, we celebrated with steaks, but as dessert, she insisted on teaching me how to get on and off the Long Island Expressway so that I could drive to her house. The trip to the British Isles never materialized, but it had already served its purpose.

When I drive now, more than thirty-five years later, whether on expeditions to freedom or journeys to fulfill burdensome responsibilities, my mother is always there, calming me in stalled traffic, beckoning me to undertake outrageous adventures, and warning me against the temptation to be a passenger in my life.

17. Eli

I adore him unconditionally, my big (and only) brother, Eli. Yet because of our age difference, he's the member of my immediate family that I have spent the least time with and don't truly know. Nine years older than me and precocious, he went off to the Massachusetts Institute of Technology when I was only seven. The day he left, I gave him a farewell gift I had made myself—a plain white string with several little plastic charms from Cracker Jack boxes attached to it. On one of his first visits home, he whipped out the string from his pocket to show me, which made me beam. After he had been in college a few months, he sent me a stuffed animal, a gray beaver, the college mascot, with "MIT" embossed on its red felt tail. That beaver had a place of honor on my bed, virtually until I went off to college, a college that I selected partly as a result of his influence. Once while my family and I were visiting him at MIT, he suggested that we go for a drive to nearby Brandeis University. At that time, Brandeis was a relatively new school and, because of its Jewish roots—it was founded by Jews and named for the first Jewish Justice of the Supreme Court, Louis Dembitz Brandeis—would be of particular interest to my parents, especially my father, who had a deep appreciation of Jewish cultural institutions and, in fact, was smitten with the school. I chose to go to Brandeis primarily for its academic excellence, but the warm memories of that drive through the campus, with Eli at the wheel, made the prospect of going there more inviting.

When I was fourteen, my brother married Judy, a bright, interesting woman he had met at a college mixer, and they moved far out on Long Island; at least, it was far out in those days: first to Huntington and then to Northport. I saw them infrequently, although somewhat more often when they began having children—three daughters in fairly rapid succession, now all accomplished women. Visiting them on my own during my adolescence always felt like a special occasion, a safe way to run away from home and not only hang out with Eli's growing family but also catch a bit of private time with this man who to me had an air of mystery. I would also have a chance to see his newest constellation of audio equipment, including speakers of ever-increasing size that I suspected would one day consume his entire living room, and to play his massive record collection. I teased him about those speakers but later would greatly appreciate the exposure he provided me to classical music. "What are we listening to? It's really neat!" I remember saying in response to hearing one of Bach's Brandenburg Concertos, the fifth, I think, for the first time. "You've never heard that before? Well, if you liked that, I've got lots more stuff to play for you." We listened for the next several hours, not only to all the Brandenburgs but also to many different recordings by Bach (driving, I fear, the rest of the family crazy). And I, a committed rock and roller, became hooked on Bach (and still am).

Eli and I were not big talkers; in that way we were both more like our quiet father and less like our more loquacious mother and Sandy. Our relationship was based less on talking than on fixing; that is, Eli was extraordinarily mechanically as well as mathematically minded and could fix virtually everything. My mother claimed that, as a little boy, he took apart everything to see how it worked; usually, but not always, he was able to put what he disassembled back together. She also claimed he was a troublemaker, getting into all kinds of mischief, but I rarely saw that side of him except for an occasional tease with a devilish look in his eye or an unexpectedly hilarious comment emerging from his usually subdued lips. Once when I was about eight, as he, Sandy, and I were finishing up a card game, he asked in a seemingly innocent tone, "Want to play fifty-two pickup?" "Sure," I responded, never realizing that the game involved his dumping the entire deck of cards on the floor for me to pick up. I might have strangled him had I not been charmed by his good-natured laughter and, more important, his willingness to join me in the pickup. In public school, Eli was a whiz in math and science, which enabled him to get accepted into MIT, where he majored in engineering. Throughout my life I have taken full advantage of his varied skills, his eagerness to help, and his ability to make me laugh.

The things I asked Eli to help me with were never that challenging, although, at least during my childhood, they sometimes required him to tap talents he never knew he had. When I was in third grade, he helped me make a book cover from colored paper and crayons for my classroom notebooks; I remember him carefully printing in black crayon the notebook title—"Myths and Legends"—and then, when I explained that the title had to be illustrated, we collectively decided on images of a spear and crown, which he drew first in pencil on scrap paper before making the final drawing in red and yellow crayon on the cover. I could only admire his straight lines and clear images, in sharp contrast to the wiggly lines and smudges I invariably would have produced with my shaky hands. When I was in sixth grade, I recruited him to make a candy lifesaver corsage for a girl in my class who was celebrating her twelfth birthday; it was no easy task tying thirteen lifesavers (one for good luck) onto a big pink bow—definitely a girl thing, which he took on without hesitation.

Perhaps my most time-demanding, costly, and exasperating request took place in my freshman year in college, when I was struggling with college calculus. During the first few days of my college career, I thought I might become a math major, but introductory calculus disabused me of that notion. During exam time I would call Eli collect from the pay phone in my dorm hallway. "Eli, I have my final the day after tomorrow, and I don't know what I'm doing. I'll fail; I know I will." "You won't fail. You'll do fine," he would always say with conviction, and then he'd go grab his copy of *Thomas' Calculus* textbook from his study; lucky for me he had used my text when he was at MIT, and he had had the forethought not to toss it out. He'd ask, "What chapters will you be tested on?" and then he'd patiently go, step by step, through the reams of calculus problems at the end of each of those chapters, carefully explaining the logic of each step. "Did you understand that? If not, we can go over it again. You can get it. It's really not that hard," he'd say calmly. And inevitably he was right, thus reinforcing my confidence and sense of competence. "You're an amazing teacher," I'd often tell him, because he truly was, with a gift for simplifying and demystifying things that at first glance seemed incomprehensible. I shudder to think what his phone bill looked like, but I did, ultimately, get an A+ in the course. Maybe I could have become a math major, but I am not sure that my relationship with my brother or my sanity would have survived.

After graduate school, when I got my own place, Eli came by to change my front door lock when my super warned that the one I had was too flimsy; the super, who had hoped to get some cash out of changing the lock himself, was not pleased. Eli also helped me set up my first answering machine, an essential tool for my budding psychotherapy practice that came packaged with unintelligible instructions in several languages; fortunately, he was able to bypass the instructions. And without him, my entrée into the world of computers would have been delayed by several years. When my father generously offered to buy me my first computer in 1985, Eli picked it out and chose the latest model at that time, an IBM XT. Once delivered, the computer remained in its box on my bedroom floor collecting dust for more than a month, largely the result of my uncertainty about whether I would ever master this complex machinery, which I feared had a mind of its own. I had begun using an electric typewriter at a fairly young age because my handwriting was totally illegible, but a computer, even though it held out the prospect of my not having to retype pages when I made errors—and I, as a perfectionist, did a lot of retyping even after Wite-Out was invented—seemed beyond me. Finally, at his insistence, he came over and set it up for me on my desk while I watched with trepidation. Eli had been using computers forever, including, when necessary, taking them apart to fix hardware problems, and assured me it was not much more difficult than an electric typewriter. He showed me how to turn the XT on and off ("just press the black button"), gave me a few basic lessons on how to use the word-processing program he had installed, and said with total confidence that I could do it, which turned out to be more or less true except for a few panicky midnight phone calls.

Many of the tasks he undertook when I was an adult required about fifteen minutes of his time to complete, but I managed to keep him around longer by taking him out to dinner. While relatively few words passed between us during those dinners, the silence was not awkward but rather comforting in its familiarity.

It was only when my parents grew old and became ill that Eli and I began to spend significant amounts of time together. Only then did we talk more extensively and move beyond the limited helper-helpee roles we had established in childhood, albeit not entirely. We would meet in one or another of our parents' hospital rooms and have lots of waiting time together to catch up— waiting for our declining parent to wake up, waiting for the doctor to show up, waiting for the inevitably bad news. I learned more about his passions and frustrations in life during those few years than I ever have before or since. For example, he told me that as a young man he had dreams about becoming an astronomer and regretted not pursuing that interest. I wondered what other dreams lay dormant.

While Eli played a tertiary role in the actual caretaking of our aging parents—my sister, Sandy, was primary, and I was her backup—we two sisters paid serious attention, if not deferred, to the opinion of our brother regarding major decisions about our parents' care. Not only had we learned our gender roles of deference far too well in childhood, but also the sexist world of our adulthood meant that male doctors talked far more readily to a son than to a daughter. Thus, Eli was an important source of the kind of comprehensive information needed for sound decision making. "Your mother has had a heart murmur for some time and will eventually need surgery," my mother's close-lipped, condescending internist explained to Eli after he had hemmed and hawed to Sandy and me about why my mother had fainted and ultimately hung up on me when I pushed him for more information. Maybe the man knew he had been remiss in not informing us months earlier, when he discovered the murmur, and didn't want to admit his oversight to "the girls." To his credit, Eli was always eager to share whatever information he gleaned from doctors and to elicit our opinions, so vital decisions about Mom's heart surgery or Dad's colostomy could be made collectively; in this area of life-and-death decision making (not to mention corsage making), Eli's gender-role training seemed less entrenched than Sandy's and mine.

A few years before my father died, Eli and Judy moved across the country to live near the headquarters of my brother's computer software business. By that time, I had become accustomed to hanging out with him at least once a week, and sometimes every day, so I experienced his departure as a real loss. He had calmed me when I was most distressed about our parents, and his humor, always unexpected and perfectly timed to the most tense moments, never failed to crack me up and relieve my stress. And then there were all those computer crises when Eli would taxi over to my place and fix the problem. Particularly in the first few years after he moved, when my father was still alive, Eli would make periodic trips to the East Coast, and we'd spend time together. Now we see each other far less often, and, as two silent types, we're not readily inclined to pick up the phone.

What I most treasure during our more recent get-togethers are our collective reminiscences about our childhood or, perhaps more important, his reminiscences of things I don't remember or never knew. Because he is nine years older, he remembers a great deal more about our family's experiences during the first four years of my life when we lived in Bensonhurst, Brooklyn, and, of course, the years before my birth. He remembers well our maternal grandparents; when I was born, my grandfather Harry, for whom I was named, had already died, and my grandmother Anna would die a few years later, when I was only a toddler. He knew them as people; I knew them as photographs.

My grandparents owned several apartment buildings on the same block in Bensonhurst, including the one where my family lived. I was fascinated by my brother's description of how he accompanied my grandfather from building to building to shovel coal from the coal bin into the furnace and then to stoke the coal. And to hear that my grandfather had a huge collection of Yiddish records that Eli adored listening to, and sometimes Eli would borrow some to play at our house, but, as he described, "I had to play them when Dad wasn't there because Dad, the Sephardic, didn't like to hear that Ashkenazi music. So Mom and I conspired to play the records when Dad was at work." I was shocked that my father, who in some ways seemed so open-minded, could be so provincial regarding his own culture.

At one point I pumped Eli for memories of my parents' reactions to the discovery that I had a disability. He remembers little except an incident one summer when we were at a hotel in the Catskills and my mother expressed concern to other relatives who were there that I was not yet walking; he thinks I was about a year old. His lack of memory is not surprising, since my disability was never a topic of conversation in my family. I've never even asked my brother what he thinks about my having a disability or whether he sees me as "disabled." I don't want to put him on the spot, or perhaps I am nervous about his answer.

Eli and I don't talk politics. He's to the right, and I'm to the left; I suspect neither of us really wants to know what the other is thinking politically. He supports my work as a disability activist, although I don't think he understands what I do. Then again, I don't understand his work with computers either. It doesn't seem to matter, this limited understanding, these politically divergent views. We don't have to "get" each other to love and support each other.

18. My Father, Myself

Once, when I was about seven or eight, my father and I took a little walk together to a local card and candy store near my elementary school to buy me something special. It felt like a wonderful treat to spend time with him alone, although I was also a bit nervous. I was always more comfortable with my mother, who was outgoing and seemed at ease with herself and me; she placed few demands on me and seemed to genuinely enjoy our being together. My father was always more stiff and formal, a sign, in hindsight, of his own discomfort with social situations and perhaps himself. Also, although he rarely disciplined me, he seemed to have high standards that put me a bit on my guard. Yet he was a bit of a softy in buying me gifts, whereas my mother was stricter, not with items she considered necessities but with frivolous things. For my father, in particular, material gifts were a comfortable way to give to his children, especially after he became successful with his business. I think it was always easier for him to express love through things rather than through words or emotional displays.

I recall little about our walk to the candy store; it was most likely uneventful, with few words passing between us. When two quiet people get together, silence prevails. When we got to the store, my father invited me to pick out whatever toy I wanted. I chose a packet of jewelry wrapped in cellophane: a heart-shaped, deep red pendant on a gold-colored chain and a matching ring. At that age, I loved pretty jewelry, even if it was fake or gaudy. It made me feel very feminine. I had my dad help me put on the jewelry right in the store, and I remember thinking that I had better hide this gift from my mother because she probably wouldn't approve. It was one of many examples of the conspiracy of silence between me and my father against my mother, although there were other times, as when my mother made a costly purchase without my father's approval, that my mother and I would conspire against my father. I was an equal-opportunity conspirator.

My father taught me how to ride a two-wheeled bicycle even though he never learned to ride himself. As a boy, he never had the money to buy a bike or the luxury of time to play with one, so he was determined that Eli, Sandy, and I should partake in what he could not. The ritual would take place every night when he came home from work. I would get up on my two-wheeler, and he would place his hand on my shoulder to keep me upright. Then he would walk, and I would pedal around the block of our house in Queens, his outstretched arm enabling me to keep my balance. After many days and weeks, perhaps it was months, of our ritual, he let go, sensing I was ready, and to my surprise, I sustained the upright position, speeding along without crashing. It was a glorious day of achievement for both of us. I don't recall ever needing him again in quite such a concrete way, although I never stopped needing him.

My father also helped me with my Spanish lessons. As a Sephardic Jew, he spoke Ladino. It was sufficiently close to Spanish that he could speak and read that language almost perfectly, although his knowledge of grammar was based more on intuition than on rules. He was pleased I was taking Spanish; it confirmed my Sephardic heritage. I was good at learning the language, but occasionally I recruited his help, in part as a way to engage this very quiet man. It was easier than chitchat. He would test me on vocabulary or help me conjugate verbs. My mother could offer no help on this score. She had studied French in school, and despite a lifetime of marriage to my father and his Ladino-speaking family, she had mastered barely a word. While she frequently expressed her desire to learn, she appeared convinced she could not, despite her considerable intelligence, and my father's relatives made little effort to encourage her or even to translate their conversations at family gatherings. Perhaps this was a deliberate ploy on their part to keep her feeling excluded; she was an outsider to this Sephardic clan, and they rarely let her forget it. I, on the other hand, looked a lot like my father's family, and they were eager to teach me the passwords. I successfully answered most of my father's queries— "How do you say the days of the week in Spanish?" "What are the Spanish words for 'today,' 'tomorrow,' and 'yesterday'?" "How do you conjugate the verbs 'ser' [to be] and 'vivir' [to live] in the 'yo'

[I] and 'usted' [you] forms, in the present and past tenses?"—for which he would praise me but sometimes with a certain degree of reservation and hesitation in his tone, if not in his choice of words. He would describe my efforts as pretty good instead of unabashedly brilliant, which, of course, is what I wanted to hear. My mother, in contrast, was more prone to hyperbole, sometimes at her own expense. In her view I was very smart, much smarter than she had ever been, a critique that blended guilt with pride and didn't necessarily feel much better than my father's assessment. Yet even imperfect praise can be gratifying and kept me returning for more.

The Spanish lessons stopped and in some ways reversed course when I reached college. I began reading Spanish literature that far exceeded my father's literary literacy; while he knew most of the words in the works I was reading, he couldn't quite put them together in ways that made sense to him. I couldn't either, but I didn't let on. Now he had nothing but unequivocal praise for a daughter who could read such books. He appropriated some of the volumes into his own library when I was finished with them, which served my purposes quite nicely, a constant reminder of his brilliant daughter. He was, in fact, a good Spanish teacher, not by his lessons but by his presence. I wanted to be like him, and studying Spanish was one of the many circuitous routes I chose.

My father was always a generous soul, at least in regard to me, his younger daughter. My mother told a different tale, but I suppose wives and daughters can evoke and provoke different types of generosity. Even with me, though, he wasn't unequivocally generous. Although he was eager to give to me, he often had his own unshakable ideas of what I needed and wanted that didn't necessarily match with my reality. One thing he loved to give to me and everyone else—including my mother and himself—was watches. You could never have too many watches. He gave me a watch for my college graduation, and my graduate school graduation, and for a host of non-occasions as well. And he owned a good dozen himself.

I don't know what it was about watches that spoke to him. He was extremely punctual—he was always on time or even a bit early for every appointment, and whenever we were going out as a family, invariably he was ready first. His sharp punctuality put him in striking contrast to most of the other members of our family. My mother and Sandy were invariably late for everything and took forever to get ready. Eli also tended to be late, but he was more reliable than my mother or my sister. I was more like my dad, generally on time and a quick dresser for an outing, although I could never beat out my dad. His gifts of watches never seemed to hurry anyone; if that was their intent, they failed. But I suspect they had more symbolic value to him.

Perhaps they were signs of achievement, or at least persistence, as they are given to an employee after thirty-five years at the job, which always seemed odd to me—at the point of retirement, why in the world would you need a watch? Maybe a symbol of orderliness. But, you know, my father had a romantic side to him. He loved to contemplate the mysteries of the universe. I remember how upset he was when we watched on TV Americans landing on the moon and sending back photographs for all of us to see. The moon until then had been a rich source of fantasy and speculation—moon in June, the dark side of the moon, mooning over your tootsie, and all that. Those photos perhaps disrupted my father's imaginary journeys. Time, too, has that mystical, intangible quality. You can try to measure it with a watch, but you can never control it. At least I never could. And time can never control me, but it can remind me of my father—every time I glance at the watch on my wrist.

19. Driving Away from Home

When I was forty-six, I ran away from home, or rather, I drove away. I bought a car without my father's guidance. Long before that time, I more than qualified for the designation of independent woman, having my own psychotherapy/consulting practice and my own place in Manhattan, but in the area of car purchase and maintenance, I remained dependent on my father. I felt oddly reassured that all of my cars had been hand-me-downs from my parents and that my father still paid my car insurance, even though there was no doubt that I could afford it. But he considered keeping me well stocked in cars and all of their trappings part of his fatherly responsibility. And I didn't protest. As a woman who was constantly being called on to prove to the world that I could do it myself, I was relieved to be able to give up responsibility for at least one area of my life. I was proudly car illiterate; my dad prided himself in being my literacy teacher. "Maybe it's the brakes," he would suggest when I'd anxiously describe some new noise. "Let's have it towed to my mechanic," he reassuringly offered when my car once dropped dead on the highway.

So when I awakened one morning to find an empty space on the street where my car should have been, I was fully prepared to have my father replace my stolen car. This time was different, though. He gallantly offered to give me his car and buy another for himself, but I knew he loved that car, and at his age, eighty-three, finding a new car as familiar and comforting as the old would be no easy trick. As he would say, "My car remembers how to get home when I don't," and the truth was, he was having increasing difficulty finding his own way. My mother, ordinarily generous, was not about to give up her new, fire-engine-red Toyota. She had waited for fifty years of married life to get the "hot red buggy" she always wanted, repeatedly deferring her own desires, settling for my father's more conservative tastes of gray or brown. Just this past year, perhaps sensing her own mortality and some weak spots in my dad's iron will, she had put her foot down. "Red car or divorce," she only half jokingly threatened. My father reluctantly conceded. How could I ask her to give up her one symbol of victory in that imbalance of power between them that had lasted half a century? And, practically speaking, how long would a brand-new, smashing red, cute little Toyota survive on the streets of Manhattan? What was I to do?

For many young (and not-so-young) people, learning to drive and owning a car are important steps on the road to independence. This is particularly true for people with disabilities, for whom the use of public transportation may be problematic if not impossible. How can you run away from home if you can't go anywhere without being transported by your family? Although I could use public transportation and had been traveling independently on buses and subways since adolescence, well before the arrival of accessible transportation in New York City, when I learned to drive in my late twenties, I did experience a new level of independence and freedom, even if I relied on my father to provide the escape vehicles. Yet I did not feel quite prepared for the degree of separation from my father that buying my own car represented. In addition, despite my feminist politics, deeply embedded gender roles made me doubt my own capacity to buy a reliable car. What did I know about cars? I could barely distinguish one from another. To make a car purchase, I felt I needed to find another father figure.

I was bemoaning my carless state to the neighborhood coffee shop owner's son, Jimmy, while he was pouring me a second cup of coffee.

"They ripped my car off right in front of my house, those bastards, and now I'm stuck without a car."

"The same thing happened to me," he responded. "I didn't think they'd do that to you, though, with your disability sticker and all. That's disgusting."

"Yeah, well, thieves don't discriminate."

I had to confess that I, too, had thought that the sticker might protect me, which is the reason that I had never bothered to use any type of car alarm. In the driving arena, being disabled had been a real asset, enabling me to obtain a disability parking permit, which let me park in "No Parking" zones and other illegal spots throughout the city. Churches were my favorite edifice. Wherever I was, I would look for the closest house of worship, take a moment to thank God, and then park right in front. The disability sticker gave me the chutzpah to keep a car in the city. I thought that in addition to providing me with multiple parking options, the permit would serve to provoke guilt in potential thieves. No such luck. Car thieves are born without guilt. Oh, how I envy them.

"I have a friend, Peter, who works at a Mitsubishi dealership. He's a nice Italian boy from a good family, and he probably can give you a great deal on a used car," Jimmy continued. I knew nothing about Mitsubishis or any other make of car for that matter. I had heard a lot about used-car dealers, none of it good, but Peter, as a highly recommended friend of a friend, sounded like a good candidate for a father figure.

When Peter and I first met, he assumed I was Italian, too, because of my Italian-sounding name and dark features. I didn't tell him any different, presuming he would be less likely to rip off a compatriot. My caution proved unnecessary. Peter turned out to be an honest, amicable guy, eager to advise but not impose. "Try a Mitsubishi Mirage. Good ratings, good price. I even sold one to my girlfriend," he told me. On the test drive, the car handled smoothly and easily. It seemed too simple, and I became panicky. How could I make a major life purchase on the basis of the opinion of the coffee shop owner's son's friend, or worse yet, on the basis of solely my own say-so? And what would my father say? Since he was helping to finance this car, I figured he was entitled to see what he was buying. I dared not buy it without him. I took him on the second of many test drives, all of which Peter accepted with good humor. Dad could find no fatal flaws, but he became fixated on an American-made car in the showroom. My father, a first-generation immigrant who had lived the American dream, from shoeshine boy to successful business owner, bought only products made in the United States. He had bought my mother a Toyota only because he thought that any car that good had to be American. He had responded to my car choice with "Mitsubishi? What's that?" I humored him by test-driving the General Motors car that had caught his eye, but the car was almost twice the price and not nearly as smooth as the Mirage; he made me promise I'd consider it.

The next day my father left a message on my answering machine: "This is Dad. I put down a deposit on a used Oldsmobile just like the one that was stolen. Okay?" Three weeks earlier I might have been thrilled. Now I was in a rage. But it hardly felt justified. After all, he was only doing his fatherly number. I had friends who would kill for a father who would buy them a car, so I decided to keep quiet and accept the gift.

Fortunately, Sandy intervened. When she happened to telephone me soon after I had heard Dad's cheery news on my answering machine, I began ranting about him. She immediately called my father and told him in no uncertain terms that he could not buy a car for me without me. He backed down, offering to cancel the Oldsmobile deal. He insisted that he could get his deposit back and that he wanted me to have the car I really wanted. I suspected that he was lying on both counts but decided to take him at his word.

Now that my father was off my case, I decided I should do some car research. I went through *Consumer Reports* and anything else I could find to make sure that the Mirage checked out. Then, at the last moment, I dragged Eli to the dealer for yet another test drive. "Buy it. It's very European, my kind of car," he reassured me, and I knew I was home free.

The day I was to pay for the car, Sandy called to suggest I wait until one of her adult sons had time to go down with me to negotiate the price. Her faith in my judgment went only so far. "Forget it," I told her. Three months had passed since I had begun this car journey, and I was tired of bringing in the male troops to rescue me. It was time to rescue myself.

The risk was getting a lemon and then having to face my father's unspoken "I told you so." Fortunately, the Mirage turned out not to be a lemon. In hindsight, I was probably not wise to rely on the advice of the coffee shop owner's son's friend. But he offered a safe rest stop on the winding road away from home. "How's the Mitsubishi?" my father would ask with regularity. "It's alive and well and living in front of my apartment building," I always answered, reading a mixture of pride and uneasiness in his face. He feared he no longer knew how to be a father. I wanted to tell him not to worry. And I need not have worried about losing my connection to him. The road away from home was not one way, and my Mitsubishi knew how to get back.

III

On Not Looking in the Mirror

20. Walk Straight!

"Why do you walk that way? What's wrong with you?" Completely self-absorbed, I was walking home from school, thinking about a chemistry exam I had just taken; it was difficult, but I felt I had done smashingly. Now my fantasies of being the top student in the class and maybe winning the Nobel Prize were interrupted by an elderly woman in an ugly brown winter coat who took me for a common cripple. I wished I could have come up with some smart-ass answer, but at the age of fifteen, any physical differences—weight, breast size, or cerebral palsy—caused extreme self-consciousness. "There's nothing wrong with me. I have a disability that affects how I walk, but it's no big deal" was the best I could come up with on a moment's notice. "Oh, I'm so sorry. Have you asked Jesus for help?" she went on. "I don't need help, and besides, I'm Jewish." When she said, "Oh, He won't mind," I thought but did not say, "But my rabbi will. And who asked you, you old battle-ax?" I abruptly crossed the street to stop the conversation.

My mother was home when I put my key in the lock, and she immediately picked up the cues. "What's wrong?" she asked, and I said, "Oh, not you, too!" and immediately relayed the "What's wrong with you" story. She responded the same way she always did to my disability tales of woe. "Well, if you'd practice walking straight in front of the mirror like I keep telling you to, people would stop staring. I don't know why you won't do it. Don't you want to walk straight?" "No, as a matter of fact I don't!" I shouted and retreated to my room, slamming the door. Once safely alone, I resumed my Nobel Prize fantasy. My studies had always offered a refuge from stupid questions and instructions on how I should walk, talk, and be "normal." Thank God I was smart, but never quite smart enough to figure out how to silence those questioners.

My mother and I had wrangled over my walking for as long as I could remember. Because of my disability, I was a disturbingly late walker. But once I was up and more or less running, my mother found my toeing in, my awkward gait more distressing than any of my other imperfections, disability-related or otherwise. She explained that she grew up with a girl who was "pigeon-toed" and the butt of endless jokes. By coaxing me to improve my walking, she hoped to save me from even worse abuse. My mother seemed so identified with her that I sometimes wondered whether my mother herself was that pigeon-toed child. Yet family stories suggested that she was extremely well coordinated and an excellent athlete. If that were so, it must have been hard for her to see herself in me, falling over my own feet the way I did. Perhaps her insistence that I walk straight was a cover for her sadness and remorse over birthing a disabled child. In fact, the "crooked" way I walked was the most immediately obvious aspect of my disability and the focus of much of the teasing by my peers. Mostly I ignored it, but sometimes I would cry; I'd vow to practice walking every day until I walked like everyone else, but such vows were short-lived.

When we moved to Queens, my mother immediately set up a full-length mirror on the far wall of the basement. The basement was a fabulous play area, full of nooks and crannies where Sandy and I would play hide-and-seek or set up a pretend school with lots of activity corners—she would insist on being the teacher. But I would always avoid that mirror. On and off, my mother would hire a physical therapist to work with me on my walking in front of the mirror. I was not a very willing patient, and invariably, my mother would dismiss the therapist—"No sense throwing good money after bad"—and drill me herself. "Walk toward the mirror. See how your toes and legs turn in? Point your toes out, more, more. Now, that's it; walk just like that." I would follow her directions exactly, while under her watchful eyes, but as soon as she left the room, I would abandon the mirror and go back to my old way of walking. "Why don't you want to walk straight?" she'd ask, totally exasperated.

I never knew how to answer her. I just knew I didn't want to walk the way she or anyone else wanted. Part of it was that I wanted her to accept me the way I was, crooked feet and all. I also knew that I could never improve my walking enough to satisfy her. She wanted me to walk like everyone else, to look "normal." That was impossible. My disability would not go away. More important, I didn't want it to go away. I had always been uncoordinated—since the day I was born. That was just the way I was and who I was. I learned to identify my body and myself partly through my jerky way of being in the world. My mother's attempt to smooth out my crookedness was tantamount to murder.

I never could or would explain why I wouldn't practice walking, but my mother must have sensed that it was a life-and-death matter because eventually she laid off. One day, the mirror mysteriously disappeared from the basement wall and found its way to the inside of a storage closet. Occasionally I would wander into that closet to fiddle with the mirror; it was a safe place to put on more makeup than my mother allowed. Not that she and I stopped fighting. We just fought about other things, like skirt lengths and padded bras. My mother never liked how I walked, but by my mid-teens, she had learned to keep her judgments to herself. Perhaps her reticence developed as she found herself facing criticism about her own body—her weight. The nasty comments never inspired her to diet—quite the contrary. She seemed to resist just as I did, determined to hold on to her soul.

I was relieved when my mother finally got off my case about my walking, but I longed for so much more from her. When that old lady in the ugly coat asked, "What's wrong with you?" I needed my mother to be there with me to confront the questioner, to challenge her authority. She seemed unable to do so. My mother agreed with the old lady's assessment and tried to change me. I wanted her to change the old lady.

21. On Not Looking
in the Mirror

Although the mirror from my childhood home was ultimately hidden in a closet, mirrors never stopped haunting and taunting me.

"How do you know how you look if you can't see yourself in the mirror?" A stupid question for me to ask a blind friend. "Others are my mirror," she explained, "telling me if my makeup is smudged or if there's a glaring stain hovering over my right boob." We both laughed. But I thought she was lucky not having to confront that internal, eternal judge at each encounter with the looking glass. At least she could choose her judges and moments of condemnation.

I don't know why I'm always shocked to see myself in a mirror. Full body or head shot, the me in the mirror doesn't seem like me at all. Surely after sixty-plus years of myriad mirror encounters, I should know what I look like. Yet I encounter a stranger each time.

Who is that woman walking in such a graceless way, with her knees and toes turned in, head and chest bent forward, body off-balance, ready to trip over a crack in the pavement, an unnoticed step, or nothing at all? Surely not me.

Why can't I claim her? Why in my mind's mirror do I see myself walking like everywoman, like any woman, like anyone but this woman?

I've never walked gracefully—never stood tall, erect, with toes pointed out—despite the prodding, pleading, cajoling of rehab doctors, physical therapists, dance instructors, and even a famous model-turned-"charm-school"-director. These were all my mother's recruits, hired to normalize an abnormal walk that wouldn't concede.

Although I fiercely battled my mother about my walk, she ultimately won. As I grew, I absorbed her vision of me as defective. Even now, although my mother is long deceased, with each encounter with the mirror, I see myself as she did, feeling her shock at the pigeon-toed girl, doomed to be tormented by the world's stares. On that score she was right—strangers and even friends don't look kindly on clumsy girls, whatever the source. The walk becomes the woman, and all else is lost.

How can I claim that girl in the mirror as me, not some shock-producing stranger? I buy a full-length mirror, not to please my mother—although she would be pleased—not to fix myself but to find myself. With focused attention, I walk up to myself repeatedly as though to make that stranger my friend. I get to know my walk, with every twist and turn and off-balance step as really mine, or so I believe. Until I am caught off guard, walking past the mirror without intent, mind elsewhere, and the defective stranger reappears. Maybe she is here for good. Maybe I need to make peace with her.

One day, I approach my reflection in the large store window of the Japanese restaurant on my corner and muse on whether I will encounter a stranger or a friend. But my musing is interrupted by a woman begging, a frequent inhabitant of this block. "Why do you walk funny?" she inquires, reminding me of that painful encounter with the elderly woman—the "battle-ax"—during childhood. Another perfect moment for my mother to coax me down the basement stairs to practice walking "normally" in front of the mirror. From some unconscious place, I find myself responding, "My crotch itches," and we both laugh. As my eyes now turn toward the store window and my reflection, "My crotch itches" becomes my mantra, the absurdity of the words somehow dulling the shock value of the unfamiliar image I see before me. I can't say that I am ready to claim that stranger, that gimpy girl who walks funny, but somehow she seems ever so slightly more recognizable, more acceptable. The image no longer has an association with only defect—I have created a counterstory, perhaps equally absurd, about a girl with a "cunt" that has been overactive and now she's paying a price. It's not the story I want to end with, not the real story about the complicated woman who is an activist, artist, lover, friend, sister, troublemaker, and, oh yes, has an odd walk, but this woman will need some time to learn what the girl knew and forgot. In the meantime, I am trying to be kind to strangers.

22. Facing My Face

I grimace, particularly when I speak but sometimes also when I smile, frown, or for other reasons move my mouth and facial muscles. Because cerebral palsy involves damage to the part of the brain affecting coordination, these muscles are poorly coordinated, at times causing my face to be contorted and literally bent out of shape. While I try to have compassion for such hardworking muscles that are doing their best to speak the words I have in mind to say or show the feelings I seek to express, for much of my life I have been disturbed by my odd expressions.

My facial expressions are hard to read, leading to misunderstandings. People sometimes ask, "Are you angry at me?" or "Are you having a bad day?" when I am feeling neither angry nor upset. My facial muscles are just going through their unpredictable contortions. Such questions can become self-fulfilling prophecies. I become angry or upset in response because I hate to be misread even when my rational self knows that the other person's confusion is understandable. Some children get frightened, as though I am going to harm them, whereas others laugh hysterically, as though my face is the funniest thing they have ever seen. I have a bit more compassion for children's reactions and, depending on the situation, offer reassurance or, if I'm in a reasonable mood, join in their laughter. Laughing at myself is very freeing. I wish I could more often find humor in the quirks of my body.

Some people project their own emotional states onto my unclear expressions. "You look scary," an emotionally fragile psychotherapy patient would tell me from time to time. When she was in a calm, focused state, my facial expressions, although strange, were not problematic. But when she felt frightened or angry, she described me as looking terrifying and threatening and could barely stand to face me. She would angle her chair away and stare out the office window, only occasionally glancing in my direction to see if my face still resembled the monsters of her childhood.

To some extent, like my patient's, my own reactions to my facial expressions vary with my emotional state—and, more broadly, how I am feeling about myself as a person/woman with a disability. Particularly when I was younger and confused disability with abnormality, my grimaces validated my deepest fear that hidden within me was a freak or monster. These fears were reinforced in the horror movies of my childhood, in which so many of the monsters had not only disabilities but also scary facial expressions that were strikingly similar to some of my own. Although it is considerably less true today, at that time, Hollywood used disability as a symbol for monstrosity; unfortunately, so did I. Some of the teasing about my disability that I received from peers served as further reinforcement. I distinctly remember a heavy-set boy in eighth grade who harassed me by imitating a much scarier version of my grimaced expression combined with an exaggerated off-balance walk; he would point at me and laughingly tell his friends about "that monster, that ape in the classroom." My friends insisted that I complain to the teacher about that boy, but I never did. I was afraid that my complaint would focus the teacher's attention on my disability, which I was so eager to hide. And part of me believed that boy's assessment.

Although these days I am less prone to consider myself a monster or a freak, when I have had a difficult day filled with stares and stupid comments or am down on myself, my contorted facial expressions can elicit those freakish feelings. More often, though, my grimaces elicit doubts about my femininity.

I find it hard to reconcile my grimaces with my image of what it means to have a feminine, attractive, sexy face. Important people in my life, including my partner, Gene, have told me that I have a pretty face. I love the compliment but don't take it seriously. I half jokingly respond that I could be pretty only when I am asleep, drugged, or dead—that is, when my facial muscles are no longer on the move. When those muscles are up and about, doing their thing, the resulting grimaces negate any pretty features that I might have.

I know I am not the only woman, disabled or not, who dislikes and devalues her own face. Some time ago, I co-led a workshop for women on body image. One of the first exercises was to hand each participant a mirror, have her look carefully at her face, and write down three features or characteristics she liked and three things she disliked. The women, the vast majority of whom were non-disabled, had no trouble identifying their facial flaws; many listed far more than three. But almost every woman was stumped by the task of identifying more than one facial feature she liked—and some could not identify even one. Even those women who most people would consider beautiful had this difficulty. My co-leader and I ultimately grouped the women in pairs so they could help each another identify their attractive features. Most women learn early on to doubt their beauty. The media tells all of us who has a beautiful face (and body); family, friends, and community reinforce those standards, which tend to be arbitrary, not to mention sexist, racist, ableist, ageist, and so forth. The women's and other human rights movements have helped some but not enough. For women who have disabilities that affect their faces, the challenges are greater. We often have real physical markings or characteristics that contradict whatever standards of facial beauty are in vogue. I once sat around with a group of women with cerebral palsy, and we played the ridiculous game of "If you could get rid of one feature of your disability, which feature would it be?" For those of us who grimaced, exorcising our grimaces won hands down—even among those who had significant limitations in other parts of their bodies.

I hate most photographs of myself because of my odd expressions; posing for photos, smiling for the camera, and saying "cheese" all put pressure on my mouth muscles to perform and conform, just the right formula to produce grimacing. I am always surprised when people show me pictures of myself that they've taken where my expressions are unflattering and expect me to like them. Surely they wouldn't do that with a nondisabled person. They would know the picture was bad. Well, maybe not. Many women I know hate photographs of themselves, claiming they are bad, whereas in my view, the photos seem perfectly fine or even flattering. I suppose as women, we dislike and disown how we look, regardless of the venue in which we see ourselves. Unfortunately, that knowledge of commonality with other women has not increased my tolerance for photos in which I am grimacing.

The best photos of me are those taken when I'm caught off guard, not posing but simply being. Gene is a pro at getting those shots. He wanders around nonchalantly and catches me when I least expect it. I yell at him, but I have to acknowledge he rarely produces a picture of me with a grimace. When I once congratulated him on his skill, he reminded me that he rarely takes posed photographs of anyone because most people, when posing for the camera, make odd or at least artificial facial expressions. How natural can anyone look when he or she is saying "cheese"? People wind up "making faces" for the camera, he explained, just as they often do when they look in the mirror, since both cameras and mirrors cause people to feel self-conscious. So my dislike of photos is not only a woman's issue but also a function of the venue.

While I like seeing images of myself without grimaces—or at least feel relieved when I see them—the reality is that I do grimace, not only when I am posing in front of the camera but also when I am going about my business in everyday life. I would like to be able to claim my grimaces as an acceptable part of myself consistent with attractiveness and womanliness. However, change is never easy.

About twenty-five years ago, I took an art class and discovered the joy of painting; I have been a painter ever since. Over the years, I have used painting and other visual arts to explore and change my negative feelings and attitudes about my disability. As part of these artistic efforts, I have created paintings of my grimacing face to see if transforming life into art would make my grimaces more palatable. But my face paintings invariably have been more disturbing than healing. These paintings all start out reasonably well. With a small mirror tacked up next to my canvas, I begin to paint first the shape of my face and then some facsimile of my eyes, eyebrows, nose, ears, and hair. I find myself creating the face of a woman who is at the very least presentable, and sometimes even attractive and appealing, even if she doesn't quite look like me. Then I get to the mouth, and despair sets in. No matter how beautiful the colors or intriguing the texture of the painted surface, the form of the mouth—those lopsided lips and the expressions they evoke—look odd and scary. The woman in the portrait, if she is a woman, is no longer presentable, and I don't want to claim her as me or even acknowledge my role as her creator.

Trying another artistic strategy, I have made collages using pieces of large black-and-white photographs of my face in which I am deliberately grimacing to the extreme; my face in those photos, by design, looks as ugly and/or monsterlike as I can make it. The diverse, at times random, ways I cut the photographs turn my mouth into a series of interesting shapes that when combined with bits and pieces from other facial features, such as an eye, nose, or eyebrow, produce a series of abstract collages that I find fascinating and appealing. When I look closely at each collage, I can see a grimace, or at least part of one, here and there, but when I stand back, the grimace has been transformed into a line, a form that is interesting and sometimes beautiful.

I find myself wondering, though, if I am cheating. Do I have to mutilate my mouth figuratively, if not literally, to make it acceptable? I return to the photographs of my grimacing face and pick the picture in which I look most grotesque. I tape that image near my computer screen to ensure that I look at it regularly. For a while the image disturbs me, and I am quick to turn away. Over time I am able to face my face without much discomfort. I recall a story an art historian friend told me about an Egyptian pharaoh with an elongated head, the result of a genetic condition, whose subjects sought to emulate the shape of his head by wearing padded hats, undergoing medical procedures, and so forth. That conversation reminds me how any bodily feature, no matter how seemingly odd or "abnormal," could become fashionable, particularly when associated with people of power or wealth. I laughingly imagine a world in which grimacing is in vogue but then realize that such a trend is probably no more ridiculous than some of the others that have pressured people, particularly women, to contort, distort, and mutilate their bodies to fit the current definition of style and beauty.

Staring at my grimacing face in the photograph has helped me if not entirely healed me. I do not necessarily like my grimaces, but I can look at and live with them without feeling monstrous or unwomanly. In fact, much of the time, I am barely aware of my grimaces—except in my most wicked moments, when I see someone staring at my face with disgust or I encounter a suspicious-looking character. At those times I think, "You want scary? I'll show you scary!" Then the capacity to grimace is a real asset.

23. Meditations on Speech and Silence

About fifteen years ago, the quality of my speech began to deteriorate—that is, I experienced a decline in my ability to produce clear speech. I always have had a speech disability, but at that time my speech became significantly harder to understand; something had shifted. Cerebral palsy is not supposed to be a progressive disability, but perhaps living (along with aging) is. With years of stress and strain, my vocal cords had become more rigid.

As my speech was deteriorating, I started to learn how speech works—by going to ear, nose, and throat (ENT) specialists who, with the latest technology, showed me exactly what my vocal cords were doing when I was speaking. The vocal cords need to be flexible so they can bend to let through the quantity of air needed to make various sounds and to sustain the flow of sounds over whole sentences. Mine refused to go with the flow—they stood straight and proud, often refusing to let me get a word in edgewise without a struggle. I watched them at work on the doctor's television screen after he did a somewhat unsettling procedure—he pushed a minuscule camera at the end of a narrow tube into my nose and down my throat. It relieved me to see that my vocal cords were not damaged, only stubborn, like the rest of me. The medical profession's proposed solution was to inject my vocal cords with Botox, a substance that would semiparalyze them so that they could no longer hold their own; hence, the air could go through without a struggle, greatly facilitating my flow of speech. As the doctors explained, the bacterium-based toxin used to make Botox is deadly in large quantities but benign in small amounts; the paralyzing effects would be temporary and would wear off in three or four months.

Two neurologists, whom I went to see for physical problems unrelated to my voice—strokelike symptoms that later vanished—both of their own accord commented on my problematic speech and suggested I pursue this Botox procedure, which at that time was relatively new. Despite my own concern about my declining speech, I was affronted by the unsolicited medical advice about my speaking capacity and my disability as a whole. I was transformed from a person who happened to have cerebral palsy to a person whose major problem was cerebral palsy. One neurologist described my "case" of cerebral palsy as something along the lines of "sadly incurable but unfortunately not fatal." I have not made a typo here—he did say "*un*fortunately *not* fatal," or some other words with the same implication; rage sometimes impedes the precision of my memory for words but not for their underlying meaning. His brash manner suggested that, of course, I would agree with his assessment: Life with cerebral palsy was tragic. I was appalled by his attitude, and in another context I would have challenged him. But he was a well-known stroke maven, and I needed him as an ally to figure out the disturbing symptoms I was having. Even though by then I had been a disability activist for many years, viewing my disability as a positive source of identity, part of me was curious about this new approach to my declining speech; clearer speech was an appealing proposition. I did not yet know the nitty-gritty of how it would work.

It was up to the ENT specialists to give me those details. I went to two such experts—the doctor who had invented the use of Botox for speech conditions and a former student of his who was less intimidating but, by his own admission, also far less experienced with the technique. Both performed the small camera through the nose and down the throat trick, which sounds worse than it actually was, and concluded that the Botox injections would most likely help and certainly couldn't hurt. It was perhaps inconceivable to them that I was hesitating. Who wouldn't take a chance to be "cured"? Me.

At that time I was not able to tolerate the thought of such an injection, so I refused to try it. Partly I was superstitious. While there are no known side effects from the use of Botox, at least no permanent ones, I could not help fearing that in my case I would experience some irreversible damage and literally be silenced forever.

I imagined I would be punished for the desire to speak freely, easily. Of course, I already had that fear and acted on it almost daily. I was silent many times when I should and could have spoken, albeit haltingly. My silence was partly out of concern that I wouldn't be understood and hence would be patronized and partly out of concern that I would be understood and rejected for what I said. In addition to fearing punishment, I hesitated to use Botox because of my irrational overidentification with my vocal cords. Forcing my vocal cords to droop seemed comparable to breaking my will. Such a prospect frightened me. Unclear speech seemed a small price for holding on to my strong, stubborn self.

The quality of my speech and others' responses to it were both very revealing. There were times when my voice was strikingly clear and other times when it was nearly incomprehensible. My emotions played a part in this, sometimes creating the illusion that I could or should have control over how I speak. In truth, I felt more like an observer than an actor. I was aware that when I was anxious, my speech deteriorated and that when my speech easily emerged from my lips, I was feeling fairly relaxed. Yet such observations did not help me regulate my speech, mainly, I guess, because I had little capacity to regulate my emotional states. And the correlation between speech and emotions was imperfect. Sometimes I was an internal wreck, yet the words readily flowed out of my mouth, and at other times I felt fairly relaxed, yet my words refused to emerge. So I placed little stake in my capacity to control my speech; I tried to reconcile myself to the reality that my speech controlled me.

The telephone was never my friend. With my deteriorating speech, it became the site of repeated humiliations. For people who didn't know me, my telephone voice elicited such jarring responses as "What's wrong?" "Are you sick?" or "Should I call 911?" These were, I suppose, reasonable responses to a voice that sounded strained and stressed. Yet such questions infuriated and silenced me, turning my strong, proud, intact self into a medical emergency. Perhaps I should have offered the person at the other end of the line an explanation of why my voice sounded the way it did, but that felt like an invasion of my privacy. I didn't make the call or pick up the ringing phone to explain that I was disabled, not dying. I usually responded to such questions with a curt "no" and then tried to proceed in a matter-of-fact way, pursuing my purpose for making the call or eliciting the caller's purpose.

Since I considered myself a disability activist, my partner, Gene, was somewhat perplexed about why I didn't use the other person's question as an opportunity to educate. "Don't you think their confusion is reasonable, given that your speech can be hard to understand?" he would ask. "No!" was my immediate response, stopping further conversation since I felt he had allied himself with the wrong party. While my voice did not evoke in him fears of my impending death, at times he found it almost as incomprehensible as unfamiliar telephone callers did, so admittedly, he was better able to understand their experience than I was. He, like the caller, put the burden on me to explain. But to say "I have a speech disability" would have created a power imbalance, since only one of us would be engaged in stigmatizing self-revelations; acknowledging my disability would run the risk of eliciting further stereotypical responses that I didn't want to hear or address. I was willing to deal with issues of power and stereotypes when I deliberately chose to take on the activist role, not when I was trying to make or receive a fucking phone call.

I remember thinking that I should be able to own my disability status on the phone in a way that felt okay, but I could not figure out how. Having impaired speech was simply a fact of my life; why couldn't I acknowledge that fact and move on? I tried to imagine the conversation.

> Caller: Are you sick? Is something wrong?
> Me: No. I have a speech disability.
> Caller: I'm sorry.

The "I'm sorry" would be as hard for me to deal with as "Are you sick?" Such a response would be judging my life as something to be sorry about rather than simply a life that could be good or bad or both or neither. And that judgment infuriated me, made me want to scream. Maybe I was judging the caller unfairly. Maybe she or he would simply say "okay" in response to my saying I had a speech disability, and then the conversation could move on. But I seriously doubted it. To most people, the news that another has a disability, speech or otherwise, would not be a neutral fact. The power dynamics in our society would transform the fact of disability into a stigma for me. If I was calling to clarify an item on my telephone bill or to report a problem with my cable service, I didn't want to have to hear in tone or words how the person on the other end of the line felt about disability or that his or her mother or best friend had a stroke that affected speech. I just wanted to do my business and be done. But such anonymity was not readily available. That partly explained why the telephone often felt more like a source of oppression than freedom.

Strangers' responses to my voice message on my answering machine were sometimes even more problematic. People made distressed or derogatory comments or left me suggestions to change my recording so I didn't sound so weird and uninviting. Half jokingly, I told Gene that one of my major motivations for even considering the Botox procedure was to be able to record an answering-machine message that did not elicit such negative responses from people who didn't know me. I also toyed with the idea of having someone else record my message, as though that person were my secretary; for example, "You have reached the office of Harilyn Rousso, etc." But somehow that felt like a cop-out. This was my voice, damn it! Why should I have to hide? I was touched by a dear friend who said in no uncertain terms that if someone called and didn't like my voice, that person could go to hell. I felt cradled by such unqualified support and wished I could be such an unconditional advocate for myself. I sometimes wondered whether I might be able to advocate more firmly if I were a man with this voice. Or not care as much about how others responded. Embedded in my feminist self was a set of antifeminist attitudes about how women should look—and sound. Part of me associated womanhood—and more specifically, sexually desirable women—with a melodious voice. Could a woman be sexy with a strained, halting, at times incomprehensible voice? It was a weird question for me to be asking. Sex appeal was not high on my list of human virtues, and I was certainly not eager to come across as sexy to total strangers on the telephone. And yet . . .

Not that I had an easy time speaking by phone or even in person with people who knew me well. The worry that my words would not come out clearly and that I would not only have to repeat them but also explain my deteriorating speech made silence or sparse words appealing options. As my speech became harder to understand, I became much less verbally communicative with Gene; he was the person I spoke with—or didn't speak with—most frequently. He was perhaps more aware of and frustrated by my deteriorating speech than any of my other intimates. He loved the telephone and was disappointed—at times annoyed—by my failure to engage in lengthy conversations. I never was an avid telephone user, even when my speech was clearer, so this disparity between our telephone preferences was not new, but it was compounded by my declining speech. At times he interpreted my silence or monosyllabic responses as my being withholding or showing lack of interest. He was not always wrong. Here was where physical and emotional factors became intertwined and confusing. He might be talking in a way that felt distant. Part of me wanted to pull him back—to me, or something I could relate to. Yet I hesitated, fearful he would get offended or angry. I avoided the anger—his, and mine, for I was angered by his distance. I hid behind my speech disability, using it as the rationale for my silence. And I tuned out, becoming distant from him, which he felt. I sometimes wondered whether if I had melodious speech, I would be able to tell him from the outset that he felt a million miles away. Doubtful. But a nice fantasy.

I had never been a big talker, even in childhood. The fact that I always had a speech disability was one explanatory factor but not the only one. I strongly identified with my father, who was exceedingly quiet. My mother, in contrast, talked easily, at times endlessly, and sometimes with an edge. During difficult exchanges with my mother or others, my father often responded with silence, a way to keep the peace. For him, silence was a survival mechanism, as it became for me. With people whom I loved the most, silence had always been one of my tools to bind the relationship together. So in some ways, although my declining speech was a great inconvenience, I also welcomed it, further insurance against ruptures in relationships.

However, I had to acknowledge that speaking what I thought and felt, even haltingly, confirmed my presence and existence out in the world in ways that silence never did. Silence never called into question my inner existence—perhaps because I was rarely silent in my head—but there was a way in which it rendered me invisible when I was out with others. I sometimes wondered how I would be or who I would be if I spoke freely, without physical or emotional hesitation. Part of the appeal of trying Botox was to begin to disengage the physical from the emotional deterrents to my speech and see what emerged. Yet I could not help wondering if this was a misguided attempt to release the silenced prisoner within. Surely, Botox alone would not transform me into a big mouth. Or would it?

Several years after I had first learned about Botox, I began going for injections with the doctor who had invented the procedure. My speech had become so difficult for others to understand that I figured death by Botox was no worse than being killed off by people's stares of misapprehension. The first time was truly terrifying—I dragged along Gene and a close friend so that they could each hold one of my very shaky hands. The injections—one into each vocal cord—were not that painful, but the machinery used to identify the most strategic location to inject the Botox made a weird grinding sound that made me jump to the ceiling precisely when I needed to be still. To this day, that sound unnerves me.

Botox shots can have varied side effects, such as breathiness, difficulties in swallowing, and the like, most, supposedly, short-lived. I've experienced many of them over the years, but that first time, I had no side effects, not a one. Even though I was told that Botox would not take effect for a couple of days, the very next day I woke up with speech that was extraordinarily clear and smooth, like I had never had in my life. God (and the disability rights movement) forgive me for this comment, but the change felt like a miracle. As an activist, I always rejected the stereotypical notion that the ultimate goal of people with disabilities is to be "cured," but I had to acknowledge that I found it glorious not to have to repeat myself, explain myself, or prove myself healthy, sane, and smart. In all fairness, I have to say that none of my other injections—the injection wears off in about three months, and you have to start over—have worked nearly as well. At the worst, I've had laryngitis for a month followed by speech only slightly clearer than it was before I began using Botox. More typical is that my speech has been somewhat clearer but not remarkably so.

Nonetheless, I've been hooked—some clarity is better than none, and there's always the hope that the next time will be like the first.

So has my clearer speech turned me into a big-time talker, able to talk back, fight back, and claim my fair share of talking time and space? Has it transformed me into a sexy woman whose every word sounds seductive? Alas, there really are no miracles. During my good days and weeks, when Botox really has made a difference, I probably talk more, but not that much more. The sense of myself as the strong, silent type does not get transformed overnight. I worry less about whether people will literally understand my words, and I get fewer requests to repeat myself and many fewer weird comments. Several friends closest to me have described a sense of relief in talking to me now—they can put aside their worries about misunderstanding what I am saying, and about asking me to repeat, worries that I never fully realized they had (my form of denial, I guess, since given the lack of clarity of my speech, why wouldn't they worry?)—and just be with me. Gene has not experienced as much relief as we had hoped. His high-frequency hearing had deteriorated, and with Botox my speech is sometimes softer and even slurred, especially right after injections, so that at times he understands me even less well than in my pre-Botox days. When it comes to communication between lovers, there is no easy fix.

Nor is there an easy fix to my lifetime of silence, in which I have learned to choose my words carefully out of concern for not only the clarity of sound but also the social acceptability of content. With a body that evokes abnormality, I have always sought to use what I say, or don't say, to prove that I'm like everyone else—that is, "normal," human. While publicly and politically, I insist that I'm as normal as I'd ever want to be, emotionally, I am not fully convinced. Now, even with clear speech, my words are sparse as I try to second-guess what other people would want or need me to say and seek to minimize a difference of opinion that might lead to rejection.

My fear of the destructive power of words—to reveal the defective self that will prove unacceptable, to explode into conflict that will lead to loss—continues to silence me. Botox has not been a remedy—only a source of clarification.

24. Daring Digits

My right hand has a mind of its own. The fingers wander of their own accord, not that I'm a pickpocket or anything. Those wiggly digits are always on the move, racing across the table or down my lover's back, ignoring my pleas for peace. I'm simply not in charge of muscles in that hand.

CP (cerebral palsy, not Communist Party) can wreak havoc on muscle control. Usually my disability is respectful, allowing me to lead the way. But my right hand refuses to comply.

Hands are useful instruments. They hug, stroke, greet, and signal farewell, draw, chisel, punch, and slap. They are powerful little creatures as long as they behave. But left on their own, they can reveal your secrets.

Those fingers fly when I am anxious, retreat and retract when I am in a depressive stupor. "Who asked you?" I want to know.

People cringe and stare when, God forbid, they try to shake that hand. I offer my left—it behaves much better. But we live in a right-handed world. People insist, although I resist. Perhaps they get what they deserve.

My right hand, a sign of defect, a source of shame. I would hide it in my pocket as a little girl, or behind my back. But Right Hand didn't like to be hidden. It would cleverly pull up the back of my skirt, revealing my slip for all the world to see. When company came, my mother would hide my hand in hers. I learned my shame from her.

As I grew up, we began to make peace, Right Hand and I. I had more important worries—where to go, who to be. It didn't have much to say about college majors, birth control, or how to protest the war. I was glad. I didn't need yet another opinion.

I became a psychotherapist. With coaxing, my right hand learned to sit quietly, listening. And then it was called to action.

I had a new patient, a survivor of abuse, who needed a hand to hold, literally, to tell her story. I offered my left, but she grabbed my right. My humiliation almost matched hers. I could barely face her. But no look of disgust showed on her face. For her, my hand in perpetual motion became a cradle that gently rocked and soothed, coaxing her words, calming her fears, healing us both.

Long after those cradling sessions, I found a lover who insisted on holding my right hand wherever we went, dismissing my protests. He hoped to cure his own physical discomfort through lessening mine. His plan worked better for me than him, I fear. My hand became more outspoken, eager for his touch. He continued to hide himself away. And then my hand discovered a new talent as vibrator, as lovemaker. My hand and I will never forget the look of ecstasy in that boy's eyes.

Now my right hand became conceited. When I began to draw and paint, Right Hand insisted on being my model. And that shameful hand became the object of my own desire. It was unique, a rare beauty—how to capture those extraordinary curves, that subtle movement on paper, in color? I sweated; the hand was cool, calm, able to hold its pose with more repose than I had ever seen. After all, it was art!

But then that damn hand wanted to be the artist, not just the subject of art. It began to make wild marks and splotches—no pattern, no beauty, signs of madness I feared. Right Hand didn't care. It *was* mad—at me, at my games of cover-up. Right Hand had a lot to say, about confinement, shame, hiding, injustice—and about pleasure, pure pleasuring in letting loose and not giving a fuck.

My right hand has a mind of its own. I am trying to follow.

25. Right-Hand Painting

Painting my right hand, the hand that had shamed me my whole life? What a ridiculous idea! No more ridiculous, I suppose, than my becoming a painter, given my poor coordination and pervasive involuntary movements. Yet now, as I look at the painting paraphernalia lovingly cluttered around me, I suspect that the artistic longing was always lurking, looking for opportunity.

As a child, I was a failure in art class. What I painted, drew, or sculpted never met my teachers' expectations, although they would patronizingly say my work was "fine," fine for a crippled girl that is. "It's lovely," I recall my second-grade teacher saying in response to my paper Easter basket, decorated with weirdly shaped Easter eggs and topped with clumsily cut, uneven fringes, before she whisked the basket away to the back of the classroom to put on a few "finishing touches." When I could, I cheated, recruiting a classmate to "fix up" my picture or art project before showing it to the teacher. "Hey, can you help me fix the eyes of my picture of this lady's head so they don't look so lopsided?" I begged Sara, the little girl with brown braids and a frilly yellow dress seated next to me, who complied, stifling a giggle. And when I was lucky enough to be able to take an art project home, I would coax Sandy, the real artist in the family, to do it for me. Once when I was in third grade, she made an extraordinarily beautiful book cover for my science notebook, with the nine planets of the solar system on the top and an ocean filled with lively creatures on the bottom, an artistic extravaganza in response to my minimalist suggestion, "How about some stars and a few fish?" I even failed at coloring pictures in coloring books. "You colored outside the lines," my mother said in an annoyed tone. "And you made one of the boy's pant legs green and the other brown. Did you ever see pants like that?" One of my few creative gestures nipped in the bud.

But in my forties, I had this yearning to do something creative with my hands, to find another way to express myself beyond words. First I tried pottery, but placing shaky hands on a pottery wheel was a formula for disaster. My rigid, unimaginative sculpture teacher, a tall, slender woman with precisely cut, short blonde hair and a long, white vinyl apron that never had a spot of clay on it, told me I had better find a way to master the wheel or find another class. I fled right after her pronouncement and almost abandoned art altogether. But Sandy, eager to share her passion for art, coaxed me to take a day-long painting workshop in which the teacher's goal was to have students enjoy the experience of painting and not worry about the end product. I had a fabulous time that day, amazed to see myself make powerful paint strokes using vibrant colors. Until that class, I had imagined myself to be a rather depressive soul, yet my painting revealed a bolder side that I very much wanted to get to know. I was hooked, and I eagerly enrolled in endless painting classes, not all with such great success—there are mean as well as fabulous art teachers out in the world—but I just kept painting, the prospect of discovering new colors and facets of myself luring me on.

At first, I began paintings without a subject in mind, following the instructions of that first, gifted art teacher. I'd apply paint and pray that something recognizable would appear. It often did—a cat, a snake, a frog. I seemed to have a whole zoo in my head, or maybe it was just that I needed company while I worked, and these creatures were easier to paint than humans and much less judgmental if I didn't get their likeness quite right. Part of what I liked about those early paintings was that they were so primitive, so childlike, as though my four-year-old self were in charge. I had feared she had died long ago, but here she was, painting with reckless abandon. Of course, I didn't let her stay totally in charge for long. Pretty soon, I began to do to her what those problematic art teachers had done to me, albeit with a bit more kindness. I began to nudge her to be more careful with her paint strokes, to use smaller paintbrushes, at least some of the time, so she'd have a little more control over the images, so they looked a bit more grown-up or, let's face it, "normal." I don't think either she or I was all that happy with this striving for normalcy, but I had learned my life lessons far too well not to apply them here as everywhere.

Later on, I found myself reminding the little girl and my adult self that I was a disability activist and that my commitment to

equal rights for disabled people "should" be reflected in my paintings, as it had in most other areas of my life. Cats, snakes, frogs,
and the host of other animals that kept appearing, including
wolves, elephants, and even dinosaurs, were not to my knowledge symbols of disability rights unless, I suppose, I painted
disabled animals, which I didn't. So as I was attempting to eliminate traces of my disability from my painting method, I began
musing on ways to integrate my disability experience into my
painting content. Too bad I couldn't leave the little girl alone,
but my attempt to paint my disability experience had some unin-
tended benefits.

I decided to start with my own disabled body, and more particularly my right hand, harder to paint than a snake but easier
to paint than other obviously disabled parts, like my crooked
walk or my facial grimaces, although I would get to those, too.
So here I was, holding my weird right hand in front of my eyes,
knuckle-side up, trying to draw a likeness on the blank white paper hanging on one of the walls in the tiny entrance hallway of
my apartment, a six- by five-foot, seven-sided space that had become my painting studio. I found myself noticing the details of
my right hand for what seemed like the first time. Usually I hid
that hand, even from myself. That hand, with its oddly shaped
fingers that were in perpetual motion and its inability to do such
basic tasks as grasping small objects without spilling them all over
the floor and shaking hands without mauling the other person,
was clearly a symbol of my disability, my difference.

Now I was confronting this freakish part of myself, or perhaps
it was confronting me. I discovered that the three middle fingers
were curved, like bananas. I was fond of bananas. The pinky was
straight but angled out quite a distance from the middle fingers,
as though it didn't want to associate with those weird, banana-
shaped digits. Suddenly I remembered that the pinkies on my father's hands angled out in a similar way, and it occurred to me
that perhaps the standoffish position of my pinky was more the result of genetics than disgust. The thumb, in contrast to the pinky,
stayed very close to the rest of the hand, not so much in solidarity,
I suspected, but because the muscles that ordinarily might move

the thumb to and fro in my hand were tight and rigid. My thumb could not have fled even if it wanted to.

These details fascinated me, like dissecting and disarming the enemy.

Now that I had carefully examined the location and shape of each digit, I was able to draw an outline of my hand on paper without much difficulty. The paper was large, eighteen by twenty-four inches, much larger than my hand, which aided in the drawing. I was able to use broad strokes with big brushes, little-girl style. The adult would have to wait her turn.

Next I began to notice what was inside the outer edges of my hand. I noted that fingernails were more rectangular than the stereotypical oval I associated with women's nails and were strikingly short, not the result of biting but of the constant motion of my fingers smashing against this surface and that, taking its toll. My knuckles were large and meaty, each consisting of what looked like a series of concentric circles drawn on my skin. The visible bone structure of my hand, extending from my wrist to the tip of each finger, reminded me of swaying tree branches, whereas the amazingly complex blood vessels covering the hand looked like intertwined rivers. Capturing these details required greater control and smaller brushes, so I put the adult in charge.

I had drawn the outer boundaries and inner details of my hand in raw and burnt umber, two neutral shades of brown. Now came the most delicious part: choosing bold, lively colors to transform this barest of drawings into a painting. Here the little girl and grown-up collaborated, using a combination of yellows and browns for the hand itself and then surrounding the hand with swirls of blue and bits of brown. Later on in my artistic journey, I would learn how to represent a three-dimensional object like a hand on a two-dimensional sheet of paper or canvas through the use of light and dark shades of paint. But at this stage I was less concerned with dimensionality than shape; I would be grateful if what I had painted had the barest resemblance to a hand. And I was delightfully surprised.

When I stepped back and took a look at my creation, I was amazed that I could immediately recognize not only a hand but my own hand. The fact that the hand didn't look "normal," that the three middle fingers looked like bananas rather than graceful, ladylike fingers, that the pinky appeared on the verge of flight, whereas the thumb was clinging for dear life to the rest of the hand did not disturb me. The pleasure of self-recognition overpowered any feelings of abnormality and self-disgust. Perhaps even more important, the painted image of the hand was no longer just a hand or even just my hand. It was a piece of artwork with a life of its own, with color and vibrancy that captured my eye and my imagination. I was drawn to look at it. And I would later discover that I wasn't alone in my interest.

When I included this piece, which I called *Self-Portrait*, in one of the first shows of my artwork, viewers were attracted to the hand and eager to comment on it. I remember one viewer said, "It looks like one of the self-portraits of Frida Kahlo." I was thrilled—the Mexican painter Frida Kahlo was one of my favorite artists—although I knew better than to take the compliment too literally. This was an early piece, and even the little girl knew that it was not great art—yet. But I did understand that this painting spoke to people in ways that had little to do with their attitudes—or mine—toward disability.

I wish I could say that this painting "cured me" of my negative attitudes toward my right hand, but it did not. Nor did the several other hand paintings I would create over the next few years. There is no quick fix for a lifetime of self-hatred, only slow healing.

26. Being Only One
Some Meditations on Solitude

Part of the pleasure I find in being alone is that I am no longer the only one who has a disability or is otherwise different. I can be more clearly myself, without reference to anyone else. Being alone offers me respite and a time to refuel without the drain of others' expectations and judgments. That may be, I realize, a glorification; I carry the world's expectations in my head, regardless of whether I am by myself or out in the world. But in the privacy of solitude, such expectations are more in the nature of background noise that I can attend to or overlook. When I choose to attend to them, I can also shape them to my liking. I can imagine being applauded and supported for my real or fantasized actions without feeling compromised. Or I can imagine being confrontational in response to expectations, demands, or criticisms that seem wrong, without fear of anger or loss. In solitude, I am much more the person I would like to be and sometimes think I could be.

When I am alone, I am not tempted to comply with others' expectations to win acceptance. I abandon the deferential mode and pay much closer attention to my own preferences. In fact, only in solitude can I risk discovering what my own preferences are. Actually, I'm extending the truth here. I often know what I do and don't like but am reluctant to acknowledge these choices in the presence of others, as though I would be judged and not be able to stand up to the judgments. I don't quite know what I fear about speaking my mind. Perhaps I am afraid that I will be abandoned for having a preference that is unacceptable or that my choice will reveal something about myself that I prefer to keep hidden, such as my real or perceived defectiveness. My desire for Mexican food when my friends or partner prefers Chinese becomes a sign of some fatal flaw within me. Such thinking seems ludicrous as I write it, yet on some emotional level I have come to believe it, perhaps the consequence of so often being the only one with the stigma of disability in the group. The message has always been to hide my different opinions or preferences, to pass, to fit in, to avoid the danger that an unacceptable truth about me may leak out unwittingly by something I've said, by my tastes or desires, inadvertently revealing my stigmatized self—that is, my defective self.

So silence, or noncommittal, nonrevealing responses are my modes of choice, or at least of safety in a group. Yet compliance can be so unsatisfying. How many Chinese dinners I have suffered through when my heart is longing for a frozen margarita. Gene is on to me, by the way. He claims to hate my deferential mode, my silence in the face of questions about where we should eat or go, what we should do, what I think or want. So extensive is my socialization, so deep my fear of exposure, that I cannot fully believe that he wants to hear my preferences not to judge me but to know me. And because his answering the questions for both of us is truly a burden for him. However, I'm not sure he totally wants to hear all I have to say to him. He says he does, and I think he thinks he does. But his sense of self is fragile in its own way—I suspect everyone's is—and sometimes seems stressed by disparities between us, although admittedly not over food preferences. I have learned my survival lessons so well, though, that my tendency toward acquiescence is global, not selective.

A poignant example comes to mind. I remember being about five or six years old, around Christmastime, waiting to see a store Santa Claus. As I waited my turn, I learned the ritual. Each child would sit on Santa's lap, tell him what she or he wanted for Christmas, and then receive a Golden children's book as a gift. When my turn came and Santa asked me what I wanted, I told him a Golden book, pointing to the pile. He assured me I'd get a book but asked me again what else I hoped Santa would put for me under the tree. I had no response. Maybe the reason was that I was a nice Jewish girl unaccustomed to celebrating Christmas, but I don't think so. Rather, I think I had already learned to squelch my desires. No, that's not quite right. I had learned to squelch publicly acknowledging my desires, as though they would be too revealing and burdensome. Silent acquiescence was a way of blending in, not calling attention to myself and hence to my differences, which I had already learned were disconcerting if not distasteful to others.

In solitude, such fears of exposure lessen, although they don't entirely disappear. My preferences feel less loaded. They are more statements of fact than mirrors into defects in my soul. I am not yet able to abandon my conviction that those defects exist, but at least they get unhooked from margaritas.

By myself, and being more fully myself, I can at times experience a level of freedom that I rarely, if ever, feel with others. Sometimes, particularly when I am painting, sometimes when I am writing, I have this momentary flash that I could be happy, that I could have a happy life. It is a shocking revelation when that thought comes to me, although it seems so trivial when I write it here. Painting and writing, when they are working, transform me—no, maybe they transport me to another place. I feel deeply connected, despite my aloneness, so that there is what I would describe as a spiritual quality to the experience. I am aware of some inner sense of joy, as though my heart were expanding, almost exploding, maybe singing. The experience is hard to capture in words. It is both elusive and very real and somehow feels within my control, as though I have made this experience, this feeling, happen. At such times I realize that I could have a happy life if I chose to. Fairly quickly after the realization, the experience is gone in all but memory, and that notion of having a happy life fades until the next time.

I don't entirely know what having a happy life means. Part of me thinks that no such thing exists, that one has happiness, sadness, and a whole range of other emotions within the context of a life so that labeling a life as "happy" or otherwise seems too all-encompassing and simplistic. Yet a notion of a happy life, a desire for it, and a fleeting experience of how it feels all reside within me.

Solitude is not a singular state, I realize. There are times when I am quite peaceful, spiritual, hopeful, as I just described. These times are the hardest to sustain; they feel stolen, secretive, unwarranted. They are delicious and alluring, yet the forces of "should" often pull me away to more mundane or practical tasks—catching up on e-mail or doing the laundry—when I may be by myself but not of myself, not much connected to what is going on inside me.

There are times of solitude when the struggles over exposure and defectiveness get reenacted. Such conflicts are easily triggered.

A pile of papers on the floor becomes symbolic of internal untidi-ness, and I rush to disperse the pile, to eliminate the clue. In the midst of my frantic efforts to restore order, I rarely grapple with that sense of internal disarray, to question it, to wonder about it. I have done much over the years to challenge and cast off the con-viction of defectiveness and freakishness that has been with me since I first became aware of people's stares of distress and disgust, probably when I was about two years old. Yet the residues remain. They are reinforced almost daily as I go out in the world or even as I stay at home and encounter a questioning or negative reac-tion to my odd-sounding voice on the telephone. The pile of un-tidy papers is not so much a reinforcement but a reminder of that negative conviction. When I feel solid internally, the pile has little symbolic value; I don't much like it even then—I do have a prefer-ence for neatness—but there is less urgency to dismantle it. Other triggers might be a wrinkled piece of clothing or a work-related task that I am having difficulty completing. I might be working on a paper or a chapter of a book, and the writing is not coming easily. Then panic sets in, and I realize I am engaged in a life-and-death struggle, that I have imbued the piece of work with my lifelong question of whether I am defective or intact. The quality of the work will determine the answer and my future. When I can catch myself and disengage the writing from my internal struggle, the paper gets written, but sometimes catching that connection takes a long time.

The defectiveness dilemma, when it does not immobilize me, intrigues me. I wonder how a physical difference got transformed into a psychic defect. I do think my disability was the starting place—not the disability per se but the reactions of others to my disability.

Before I became overwhelmed by society's view of my body as different, as deficient, in need of "fixing," I believe I had a sense of my body as simply being my body, the body I was born with, whole, intact, complete. My conflict about my body—and ulti-mately, myself—grew out of these contradictory views: Internally, I felt okay about my body, but I kept getting messages from the outside world that it was not okay. It is easier for me to hold on to that internal, intact view in solitude, which explains why I find being alone so appealing, although those negative mirrors are always lurking even in the privacy of my own room. In my happiest moments, those mirrors are not so much hidden or absent but transformed. My paintings, my writings become my mirrors, reflecting all that I am and hope to become—a work of art, a creative life in process, a woman open to herself without fear or judgment.

IV

What's a Woman?

27. What's a Woman?

At age twenty-four, although anatomically female, I did not feel very womanly. So when a left-leaning friend coaxed me to go with her to an organizing meeting for women's consciousness-raising groups in Washington, D.C., where we were both living and working at the time, I expected to be revealed as a fraud. I never measured up to traditional images of beauty. I was uncoordinated, with an awkward gait and slightly slurred speech; real women were graceful and melodious. But more than my appearance, the fact that I had never been with a man confirmed my nonwoman status. Not only had I not slept with a man; I hadn't even dated one. From what I could glean, being a woman seemed very much dependent on being able to catch a man. And women's consciousness-raising groups appeared to be a protest against oppression by men once you caught them, or they caught you. Knowing nothing about such things, I vowed to keep my mouth shut.

At the meeting, women living in the same geographic area gathered to form their own groups. Here was where my friend and I parted company, to my chagrin, since we lived on opposite ends of the city. I walked to my group's meeting place slowly, monitoring each step with the hope that my uncoordinated gait would be less obvious. I was the only woman with a visible disability in the room, the only misfit, or at least the most obvious one.

When I arrived at the gathering spot for my area, all of us began first by floundering and then by introducing ourselves. I surprised myself by immediately talking about the very facts about my body that a few minutes earlier I had sought to hide. And I acknowledged real doubts about my womanhood. No one seemed freaked out by my tale of difference. Several other women had their own tales.

For example, there was Martha: "I was abandoned in the hospital when I was born. I have always felt unlovable."

And Estelle: "I jumped into marriage right after high school to escape my parents' house. Now I have two young children and a miserable marriage. I must have some fatal flaw to have gotten into this situation."

And Susan: "I'm a college freshman, and all the other girls have so much more sexual experience than me. I feel out of place, like a walking disaster."

And Betty: "I'm overweight. People treat me like a fat pig."

It was a quiet revelation to discover how the "What's wrong with me?" theme seemed to punctuate each of our lives as women. And thus began our political consciousness and, equally significant, our bonding.

We met every week at one another's houses, drawn together by geography and our collective self-doubts. We laughed when we discovered how each of us hated some part of our body: our boobs, our waistlines, our facial features. I remember my initial terror when Martha, the woman who had been abandoned at birth, insisted on holding and stroking my right hand, which had always been a source of great shame to me because my fingers were constantly in motion and out of control. "I never let anyone touch that hand," I explained. "Well then, this stroking is long overdue," said unhappily married Estelle. "Let's give your hand a coming-out party," suggested Betty, the woman struggling with her weight. Betty knew as much as I did about hiding. She allowed herself to wear only black, and she avoided most social events. We took her on a shopping spree soon after the "right hand" session and encouraged her to buy an outrageous orange-flowered dress, which she eventually wore to a singles' event. I went with her, both of us deciding that two freaks were better than one.

One night, when we were meeting at Estelle's house, her husband sat down and began giving us a diatribe on how the women's movement was changing society. He seemed unwilling to leave. "So what are you doing to prepare yourself for the revolution?" I heard jump out of my mouth without my conscious consent. He laughed awkwardly and then immediately excused himself. My sisters-in-crime applauded. I found myself wondering how I could react so strongly to sexist oppression when I thought I had never experienced any.

Another night, we decided to go to a porno flick to see what all the fuss was about. We drove there in Estelle's small, beat-up convertible, which seated at best three and we were five. So we put the top down, and two of us sat on the rear of the car, with our legs hanging over the back seat. Then we heard the police siren. "There's a law against hanging out of the car like that. Don't you girls know that?" two male police officers pontificated after pulling us over. Their eyes shifted from one to another of us, rating our sexual succulence. Our collective rage was rising, but we resisted the temptation to talk back, other than Estelle's statement: "I think at our age, we no longer qualify as 'girls.' You can call us 'women.'"

Catching the movie seemed preferable to a trip to the police station, especially with those characters. The movie was worth the silence. *A History of the Blue Movie* provided snippets of major porn films made since time began, or rather, since films began. It was a smorgasbord of lust and disgust that at differing moments made at least some of us want to puke, while others of us had our nipples hardened against our will. Upon leaving, Susan made the understatement of the year: "Well, that film was an experience!" A complicated experience at that. Afterward, we talked about both the degrading images of women in the film and the lack of sexual pleasure in our lives.

I, of course, had to confess that I had never had sex, which reassured Susan, who as a young college student, was only one or two sexual encounters ahead of me. "Of course, you've had sex," Martha insisted to me. "What about masturbation?" What about masturbation indeed? My total ignorance, which, thank God, Susan shared, precipitated a group visit to the local drugstore to buy Susan and me vibrators. I was more than a little embarrassed when the blushing male clerk showed us the various models from the glassed-in, locked-up case. But my sisters kept me on task, and on the basis of their collective wisdom, I made my purchase. Susan couldn't bear the prospect, so we excused her temporarily, because of her youth. But at the next meeting, after I had spent several delicious nights vibrating myself into seventh heaven, I convinced her that a vibrator would be one of the most important purchases of her life. I took her back to the drugstore the next day.

Good things do not last forever, but perhaps they don't have to. Susan was the first to leave the group when she returned home for summer vacation, but not before she asked for advice on where to hide her vibrator from her mother. "How about in your paint box?" I suggested, remembering that she was majoring in fine arts. I moved to another city and, fortunately, being older, didn't have to worry about hiding my desires in disguised containers. They were out in the open now, and so was I.

28. He Was the One

I don't recall how the conversation began. I was in my mid-twenties, visiting with my parents at their house in Long Island. My mother was off somewhere, probably shopping, one of her favorite activities, which left my father and me home alone to keep each other company. Since we were both nontalkers, that meant our sitting quietly together—my father engrossed in the newspaper, I with my head in a book—or perhaps our watching TV together. I suppose I must have looked blue or moody, not terribly unusual for me those days, or even today. My dad, though, for all his noncommunication, was quite good at reading nonverbal cues—particularly mine, less so those of my mother, who could be about to explode at him and he'd seem not to notice. Maybe he did pick up on her cues as well as he picked up on mine, but dealing with hers was harder. I rarely threatened him. I only adored him.

So when he stated, "I know why you are depressed," I wasn't surprised that he had noticed my moodiness but rather startled at his claim to know the reason for it. Even I didn't know why I was down, other than the pervasive malaise that seemed part of my temperament. "Really? Why do you think I'm depressed?" I inquired, curious to learn his explanation. It could shortcut my therapy and save me a lot of money.

"No boyfriends. No men want to go out with you, like on dates," he said. I was flummoxed, not because he was necessarily wrong—it was upsetting to be in my mid-twenties and never to have had a single date in my life—but rather because we had never, ever talked about boyfriends and dates. My father was one of those modest, chaste types, so I doubted that he talked all that much about dating or sex with anyone, much less his children—although in thinking it over, I did recall snippets of conversations that he had had with Eli and Sandy, mainly words of warning, and there was one angry exchange with Sandy when she came home late from a date. But with me, not a word. I suppose he assumed, like I did, that dating and boyfriends were off the table for me, given my disability, so there wasn't anything to think about or say. But clearly he had been thinking about my romantic potential in a way that disheartened me even though I shared his pessimism. Reluctantly I proceeded with the conversation. "Why do you think men don't want to go out with me?" My father hemmed and hawed for a while, so I thought I'd put him out of his misery. "Do you think men don't want to go out with me because of my disability?" "Yes, that's it," he replied. I don't know why his answer disturbed me. I thought the same thing. I suppose it was doubly disturbing to hear my worst fears validated by the man who had always been my greatest supporter and admirer, who always told me I could do anything I chose to do.

Then I took a deep breath and asked the question that I really didn't want to have him answer. "Do you think you would want to go out with a woman with a disability?" "No, I guess I wouldn't," he responded without hesitation. I abruptly left the room. And at that moment, I knew where many of my self-doubts about my ability to attract a partner had come from and why I had never attempted to date. In the back of my mind, I had always blamed my mother. She was the safer target. But he was the one. Without a word.

29. Blank Page

My silence becomes a blank page on which you imagine who I am. Your vision, distorted though it may be, feels safer than my presenting myself as I really am. From a position of silence, I can disavow your vision of me as yours. But if I speak and you still come to the same conclusion or worse, then I may feel compelled to accept your conclusion. Your fears become my self.

30. Buying the Wedding Dress

It was a traditional Jewish family ritual—the married women in the family going shopping with the bride-to-be to buy her wedding dress. I had been sheltered from knowing about this ritual, perhaps because no one ever expected me to get married. Because my body moved in ways far removed from traditional standards of feminine beauty, I consistently got the message that no man would ever want me. It became a self-fulfilling prophecy until, at age thirty-seven, I met Michael, who convinced me I was the most beautiful, desirable, sexy woman in the world and that my strange movements were exotic, not weird.

So there I was, one early July Saturday, surrounded by my mother and Sandy, who had been married for more than two decades, going from bridal shop to bridal shop in one of those wedding malls in Long Island, seeking the dress that would transform me into a "real" woman, Michael's wife, on October 7. There were only three months to go, so I couldn't afford to be too choosy. I had to pick something off the rack that needed, at most, minor alterations. I didn't realize that I had a picture of the ideal wedding dress lying dormant in my brain, but the image emerged full blown as soon as I started trying on dresses. As a woman who favored jeans and simple styles, I was shocked to discover my own preference for lace and frills, tight waists, and wide skirts. The four-year-old who had played with bride dolls before she discovered there would be no groom was at last in charge, unhampered by the restrained tastes of her grown-up self. My mother, Sandy, and I let the little girl rule, and she decided on an off-white satin gown with lace covered with pearls throughout the broad skirt and deliciously smooth-to-the-touch satin at the waist and sleeves. My reflection in the mirror did not exactly match the one in that four-year-old's head—my body was still less than perfectly coordinated—but I felt more beautiful and womanly than I ever had before. I had my first dress fitting and tried on different crowns of flowers that helped complete that image of myself as a princess.

We went out for a bite after my mother made the sizable down payment. I felt totally satiated despite the slim pickings at the dingy coffee shop around the corner from the bridal store, so delicious was that image of myself in that long white dress.

I called my groom-to-be from the restaurant, and although he tried to show happiness about my purchase, I couldn't help noting some distance in his voice. I attributed this to prenuptial anxiety, but I had a visceral feeling of loss, as though the Polaroid picture of myself in the wedding dress was starting to fade.

When I saw Michael that night, he suggested that we not go anywhere special for dinner, an odd request given the events of the day. I found myself in yet another bleak coffee shop. I don't recall how the conversation started, but fairly soon after we got to the restaurant and had ordered our cheeseburgers, he came out with a litany of complaints. "You don't read the *New Yorker*. That magazine is such an important part of my life. It makes me feel lonely to think of marrying someone who doesn't like the *New Yorker*." And "You're not into philosophy like I am. How can I share my ideas, my passion?" Unprepared, I was unable to defend myself or to question the legitimacy of his complaints. In my state of disorientation, I was falling back on old truths about myself. In fact, they were myths, but they felt like truths. In my mind, what he was saying was that there was something deeply and basically wrong with me, a feeling I had developed as a child as the result of people's repeated pointing, staring, and asking what was wrong with me. The world's reflection of me as defective had made me assume I would never marry. And Michael's supposed love for me had made me question that image for perhaps the first time.

In hindsight, it is absurd to think that my not reading the *New Yorker* could transform me back into a freak, but it had that effect, at least temporarily. "Are you sure he really asked you to marry him?" my dad inquired when I told him the wedding was off. "That bastard!" was the immediate response of my mother, always my advocate. "Thank God!" is what the three of us might have said had we known then what I learned later about Michael's history of near marriages before and after his encounter with me.

Many wedding dresses had been bought and abandoned after early fittings at bridal shops, even by some women who read the *New Yorker*, I suspect.

That image of myself in the wedding gown has lived on, although it has lost some of its sharpness after almost thirty years. I did see a reflection of a real woman, not a freak, when I gazed into the mirror that day, and that woman was in me, not in the looking glass. She goes in and out of my awareness now, but I know she is there. She has a disability, and she is whole.

31. First Date

He had answered my ad in the *New York Review of Books*. This was to be our first date, after exchanging letters and talking on the phone a couple of times. For our meeting, I picked a restaurant in my neighborhood that I liked, Knickerbocker, one that I had gone to many times, including on other first dates with men I had met through the *Review*. It was a public place and therefore reasonably safe, an easy escape if the man I was meeting turned out to be a dangerous character. Fortunately, none of the men I had met there over the months had caused me to flee, at least none so far. I got there a bit late, and he was already waiting outside, giving me a chance to look him over from afar as I walked down the street toward him. He was tall, slender, bearded, hippylike, cute, and definitely appealing, even more so as I got closer. As he saw me, he offered a friendly smile, which was a relief. I always worry about men's first reactions to me and my disability. Having a disability is a stigma out in the world in general but even more so in romantic relationships. Many men prefer women who in some ways meet their idealized image of attractiveness, beauty, or sexiness. A woman with my disability rarely fits that image. He knew I had a disability—I had put it in my ad—but it is one thing to read the word *disability* and quite another to encounter a real person with that disability. More than one man had ended our first date rather abruptly, with a look of discomfort, disgust, or displeasure in his eyes. I can't be sure that the reaction was based solely on my disability. I'm no fool—well, maybe I am, but not in this way. I know I have other physical and personality characteristics that may be displeasing to others. But with this man, Gene Brown, who is now and has been my life partner and love of my life for more than twenty-five years, there was a smile that seemed real and welcoming.

We went into the restaurant and ordered: cheeseburgers and french fries. Those were the days when we could both eat such things without getting killer heartburns. Once we ordered, we made small talk, each of us trying to become more comfortable with the stranger across the table. We started with real estate, a typical New York City topic: his rent-controlled apartment in Brooklyn Heights that many would kill for, my rent-stabilized apartment in Greenwich Village that might not warrant murder but definitely was a steal by most standards. I asked about his work, admiring his capacity to be a freelance writer, not realizing until later in my own career the precariousness and pitfalls of the freelance life. "I've written books on everything you can imagine, from computers to sports to child safety," he explained. "But the topics are rarely of my choosing. Sometimes I get stuck writing books that turn my stomach. For example, I've done a few that promote capitalism, for which I, of course, got paid pittance, making me feel like an exploited worker supporting a system I despise." I was relieved to discover I had a lefty in my midst. "I consider myself an anarchist," he clarified, going on to describe some of his many political activities, including his participation in the 1963 March on Washington, and the beating he took while joining in protests in the late 1960s at Columbia University, where he had been a student. I, in turn, described my work in the disability rights movement, about which Gene acknowledged knowing relatively little but showed interest and an eagerness to learn. "You actually get paid for being an activist?" he asked with amazement, when I described how I obtained a grant to start a mentoring project for adolescent girls with disabilities that promoted empowerment.

I'm not sure what led us to discuss our favorite old movies, but that topic initially put me in a panic. I loved old movies but had no memory for their titles or who played the starring roles; I feared making a fool of myself. "One of my favorites is about a love affair that starts on a cruise ship. I think Cary Grant is in it, but I can't remember the title," I said apologetically. "*An Affair to Remember* starring Cary Grant and Deborah Kerr. It came out in 1957, I think, when I was fifteen; I remember what movie theater I saw it in, in my neighborhood in Jackson Heights. That's one of my favorites, too," he said in a kindly way, apparently willing to serve as our collective memory with no judgments. He went on to describe a few of his other favorite movies, with their dates, directors, stars, and so forth, and then stopped himself, acknowledging his list could go on forever because he loved movies, especially old ones, which delighted me. And then there was the cat connection. "I wish you could have met Mumford," he said, his cat named after Lewis Mumford, the subject of his master's thesis. "My next-door neighbor had two cats, brothers, and when he decided he couldn't keep both, he convinced me to take one of them for a day on a 'trial basis.' That evening, while I was on my bed, talking on the phone, the cat jumped on my bed and curled up on my chest. I was sold. Of course, he never did that again, but he found endless other ways to win me over. He had such good taste: he loved Häagen-Dazs—vanilla." I in turn described my love affair with Desi, the stray black cat that my mother reluctantly let me adopt when I was nine, named by Eli, then an engineering student, after "decibel," a logarithmic unit of measurement used in electronics and acoustics. "Desi invariable hung out on my bed, purring, kneading my chest, and demanding attention. He also had very refined culinary tastes," I explained to Gene. "He'd eat only Bumble Bee tuna fish, never Chicken of the Sea, and nothing but a raw egg in the morning."

As our conversation continued, we repeatedly discovered common interests and, most intriguingly, friends in common, once or twice removed—I knew through some of my friends the names of some of his friends, and vice versa. One of my best friends, Roberta, who had been heavily involved in the civil rights movement in the South during the 1960s and had on more than one occasion put her life on the line, knew through some of her political work in the city one of Gene's best friends, Robert, who was extensively involved in various leftist activities.

Then we got to the elephant in the room, at least on my side of the table. He did not raise the topic of my disability directly, but even his backhanded approach was more honest than I was accustomed to on first dates. I was slightly taken aback but had to admire the man's courage. Apropos of nothing I can recall, Gene said, "One of my favorite uncles, Julius, was almost deaf. He used to wear this old-fashioned hearing aid, a big box around his neck that amplified the sound. He saved me, really defended me, when my father gave me a hard time. When I was in graduate school and things got impossible at home, he even let me move in with him. One good thing about living with him was that when he took off his hearing aid to go to sleep, he couldn't hear a thing, so I could turn up the TV as loud as I wanted." "Sounds like a terrific guy," I said and was about to ask more about Gene's relationship with his dad, which would undoubtedly have moved us away from the disability theme and put me, the psychotherapist, in a more familiar realm, but Gene was determined. "One of my best friends has rheumatoid arthritis. He's been having a bit more trouble walking lately and has started using a cane, which hasn't been easy. But he is really into taking good care of himself and exercising. I should follow his lead." I was working on a response when Gene went on. "When I used to work in the Columbia University Bookstore, my boss had had polio as a child. I barely noticed his disability, except when we would walk up the stairs, and I'd see him pulling up his leg. But he did everything, even played tennis. I don't think he saw himself as disabled." My head was spinning by this point. I was grateful that his "some of my best friends" stories were basically positive, no telethon talk here. Some of what he described raised questions about "passing" and disability identity that in another context, in my disability activist role, I might have pursued. But we were here on a first date, and he appeared to be telling me these stories to get to know more about me, the woman, not my disability politics. As Gene would later tell me, he didn't quite know what to make of the fact that here he was sitting with a woman who, on the one hand, he found attractive but, on the other hand, had a set of disability characteristics that were unfamiliar and unsettling. Gene is a fabulous conversationalist, so he used his gift with words to talk around and through his confusion.

I wish I had had the courage to redirect the conversation, to ask if there were some things he would like to know about my disability. I didn't. As a disability activist, I was certainly no longer in the closet. But as a dating partner, I was still a novice, particularly concerning whether and how to discuss my disability. I simply hadn't dated enough to come up with a strategy that felt comfortable to me. Should I say right off the bat, "Hello, my name is Harilyn Rousso; I have cerebral palsy, a disability I've had since birth that involves damage to the motor part of the brain, and yes, I can have sex"? Or should I keep my mouth shut until the man has a chance to get to know me more fully, beyond my disability, and then answer any questions he has, assuming he hasn't already fled out of anxiety or discomfort? I've had the experience of telling too much too soon—and waiting too long to say too little. I've rarely gotten it just right.

My last big romance, which had ended a year or two before I met Gene, was with Michael, a man whom I might now describe as having had a disability fetish. He had been preoccupied with dating disabled women. And my ability to be open and honest about my disability, which at the time had felt like such a pleasure, had reinforced his problem. From the moment I met him, Gene seemed infinitely sane, deliciously quirky and idiosyncratic but sound and solid, at least as far as I could tell on a first date. For example, at one point, as our conversation drifted to finances, he noted, "I'd rather have lots of books and records around me than lots of money. Good thing," he went on. "I earn much less income than virtually any of my friends. I'm not your typical American. I've never owned a house or a car. I don't and never would put a dime in the stock market. The market is going to crash soon, by the way." (And a year later it did.) At that point, I made a mental note not to tell him my annual income, modest by most standards but definitely not by his, and prayed he was wrong about the stock market. (If only I had listened.) I also wondered how he survived financially. But he quickly explained that despite his meager annual income, he had saved a significant amount of money—parked in CDs, of course—enough to provide him with considerable security to live a fairly comfortable life, surrounded by wall-to-wall books and records that gave him much comfort and pleasure. "Of course," he went on, "I rarely have dinner at Lutèce, or any other high-end restaurant in the city, but I can whip up a delicious bowl of spaghetti with white clam sauce big enough to share with you." A man after my own heart and stomach: I loved spaghetti and hadn't even heard of Lutèce. His attitudes toward money were not typical of those of most men I encountered, but they seemed well thought out, grounded in his values, and reflected in his actions. While his efforts to discuss my disability were less straightforward than our discussion of most other things—which was understandable, given that he likely had never before dated a disabled woman—they reflected a very appealing combination of honest curiosity, respectfulness, good will, and charm. Eventually, if he stuck around, which by two bites into our cheeseburgers I was hoping he would, I would be able to reveal more to him. Not all, mind you. I'm still working on revealing all of me to myself, much less to him, and I'm not sure I'll ever achieve complete self-disclosure, but I was definitely hoping to have the opportunity to reveal more to him—about my disability and everything else.

Fairly soon, we moved on to other personal things like earlier relationships in our lives. "I was married once, about fifteen years ago," he said. "We had so little in common, I can't imagine why we married. But that was a lifetime ago, and I was a different person. The breakup was brutal. Sent me into therapy, which was one of the few good things that came out of the marriage— that and the rent-controlled apartment where I stayed after she moved out." "Sounds devastating," I said, again impressed by his honesty and happy to discover that he had been in therapy. Perhaps because of my psychotherapy training or maybe just because I was a New Yorker—in those days, everyone in the city was in therapy—I was wary of people who had never been in therapy. I feared they might not know themselves very well and could mistreat others without much awareness. That was certainly the case with my last boyfriend, whom I then talked about with Gene. "I almost got married once, a couple of years ago. The man, Michael, was extremely charming and bright but also unstable and unreliable, doing hurtful things without giving them a second thought. He proposed to me and then broke it off the day I bought my wedding dress. I later discovered he liked to propose, especially to disabled women, but could never make a commitment. That relationship was quite a heartbreak for me. I was in therapy at the time, but a lot of the turmoil happened in August when my therapist was away. Fortunately, I had a lot of good friends around." "That sounds dreadful," Gene said, "but you are lucky you didn't marry him. Then you probably would have had to go through a divorce, which, believe me, would have made the situation worse." He was right, of course.

After sharing our collective traumas, one of us asked the other, "So how do you like meeting people through personal ads?" We both laughed. "I've met some really nice people but occasionally had some weird encounters," I explained. "One man soon into our first date asked how I'd feel about spanking him with a hairbrush when we got around to having sex. When I said I like to get to know someone before I have sex, and that in any case, I'm not into hairbrushes, the evening fizzled fairly quickly." "I've had a few weird encounters, too," Gene said, "but I'm not sure I could top that. I don't like hairbrushes either, by the way."

Throughout, there was an easy flow of conversation, with moments of connection, of laughter, of pleasure in being in each other's company. It occurred to me that had I met Gene in another context, say, at a political demonstration, I could imagine our becoming good friends. In addition to the attraction, I simply liked him, and I found that reassuring. I wasn't looking for a love-at-first-sight encounter that might cloud my judgment and take me down a disastrous road; I'd done that once with Michael. I much preferred finding someone whom I could envision as a friend and then see what else might happen.

Our first date was on the afternoon of the first night of Passover. After our lunch we both headed off to separate Passover Seders with family and friends, another common bond. We acknowledged having had a good time with each other and talked about meeting again. Having had a number of these "newspaper ad" dates, I thought I was pretty good at picking up the vibes and definitely expected to hear from him.

Days, weeks, and finally months passed without a word from him. I was perplexed, wondering if I had totally misjudged his reactions to me on that first date, whether my hopefulness had all been wishful thinking. Finally, figuring I had nothing to lose, I dropped him a note saying how much I enjoyed our lunch. He called soon after, sounding just as friendly and engaging as I remembered him, explaining he had been working on a book project with a tight deadline and hadn't had much time to do anything else. I decided to believe him, although I had my doubts. No time for even a phone call?

We agreed to meet for dinner, and over the next few months— it was summertime—we had dinner together quite a few times. Each get-together followed a pattern: an early-evening date during the week at one or another restaurant around my neighborhood, often his choice—he knew an amazing number of delicious yet inexpensive places that I had never been to, even though I had lived in the area for more than a decade. He introduced me to the Magic Carpet, a fabulous Middle Eastern restaurant where we shared a plate of hummus, and then I had an intoxicatingly delicious vegetarian rice dish, while he had a perfectly seasoned lamb dish that made my mouth water when he gave me a taste. And Gene, spaghetti maven that he was, knew several inexpensive Italian restaurants on Bleecker Street as well as one way over on the West Side Highway where you could look across the Hudson River to New Jersey, if you were foolish enough to want to see that state. Over dinner we'd have casual, interesting conversations: "How's your franchise book going?" I inquired on one occasion. "It's driving me crazy, taking endless hours for very little money. The deadline is a killer," he responded and then asked, "How's your mentoring project?" "We're doing some neat things with the girls. Last week we brought them to the lab where one of the mentors, a neurochemist, works, and the girls were both entranced and horrified by her rat experiments." "That's great for the girls, but I suspect I'd be horrified, too. I'm not a big rat fan. Mice, on the other hand, are cute. Ever seen one?" he inquired. "Of course! I live in New York," I joked. After we ate, we would wander around the nooks and crannies of West Greenwich Village, laughing at the odd intersections of some of the streets— "Look here!" Gene joked on one occasion. "West Twelfth Street meets West Fourth Street. No wonder everyone gets lost in the Village." We would sometimes stop in front of an old brownstone house for sale, admiring its beauty and quaintness, challenging each other to guess the selling price, which we were sure would be more than either of our lifetime incomes.

Invariably, we'd end up at an Italian storefront near the intersection of Bleecker Street and Sixth Avenue, where we'd buy

Italian ices, usually chocolate, and meander toward the Seventh Avenue subway that Gene would take to go home. Our dinners were easy, casual, and friendly but also dispassionate. I enjoyed them but was also perplexed by them. We were clearly becoming friends, or at least were friendly toward each other, but the friendship was not deepening or changing into the romance I had hoped for. Whatever sparks I had felt for him initially were cooling and dying. Paranoid as I often was, I kept wondering whether there was a disability angle to his distance; was he turned off, put off, or put out because of some aspect of my disability? He never seemed flummoxed or uncomfortable when I tripped or was hard to understand or made what seemed to me weird facial expressions. I also wondered if it was something about my personality. He was philosophically on the pessimistic side—pessimistic about the economy, about politics, about life. I am not by nature bright and cheery, but I often found myself attempting to temper his pessimism, a carryover, I think, from my family relationships when I felt compelled to talk my mother out of her periodic depressed or upset moods, never with success, mind you. Maybe I was too upbeat for him, an odd self-assessment for someone who had more than her share of depressive periods. I couldn't make sense of it all and decided maybe I just needed to let this relationship go.

At the end of the summer, I went to Santa Fe, New Mexico, on vacation with my civil rights activist friend Roberta. We often took summer vacations together, each of us pleased to have a compatible traveling companion, and invariably we had great fun. This trip was no exception as we meandered through the annual Indian Market, visited the pueblos of well-known Native American pottery makers, and shared pitchers full of peach, strawberry, and watermelon margaritas. In those days I tended to send postcards to family and friends when I was away, and as an afterthought I included Gene in my list of postcard recipients. Gene would later describe my postcard message as "brief and noncommittal," reflecting my ambivalence about the relationship. It went something along the lines of "In Santa Fe, home of several cultures, variously intertwined. Hope all is well." I think the postcards I sent even to distant relatives had a bit more heart. Sometime after I got back from vacation, I got a Jewish New Year's card from him, which surprised and energized me. With some apprehension, I called him, wondering what I was letting myself in for. Well, at least it was no longer August, and my therapist was back from vacation, I figured. "I'm so glad you called," were the first words out of his mouth. I've really missed seeing you and would like to get together." He went on: "I can't talk long now. My birthday is coming up soon, and my friend is cooking me dinner tonight. I'm already late. Can I call you back?" "Sure. Happy birthday! How about I take you out to dinner for your birthday?" I responded, wondering why I was offering to treat him to dinner when I had been feeling so lukewarm about him. "That's lovely. Thank you so much. But we have to wait until the World Series is over. The Mets are playing, you know. I can't miss a game." Well, at least I knew who my competition was at that moment. I could live with that. When he called me back, we finalized our postseries dinner plans. I decided to take him to Whole Wheat 'N Wild Berrys, my favorite natural food restaurant, which was down my block on Tenth Street off Sixth Avenue. If all else failed, I figured I'd get a scrumptious meal out of the deal. I needn't have worried.

That birthday dinner was one of those unexpectedly magical evenings in the sense that I was so deeply engaged in conversation with this man that I lost total track of time and place. When I looked at my watch as we scraped off the last crumbs of the peanut butter pie with whipped cream that we were sharing, three hours had passed and we were among the last customers in the restaurant, the waitperson repeatedly pacing back and forth alongside our table so he could collect his tip and go home. There was nothing overtly romantic or seductive going on between us, yet there was an intensity, a pull that seemed to take me over. That was the night I fell in love with Gene. Clearly, something had profoundly changed in our relationship. I didn't understand the change, but I felt it.

Gene called me a day or two later to thank me for the dinner and to ask if I'd like to go with him the following Saturday night to the South Street Seaport. "I haven't been to the Seaport since it was renovated. Have you?" he inquired. "I've never been to the Seaport period, a shameful confession for native New Yorker," I responded. "Well, you're in luck. I'm a historian, so I can tell you all about how it used to be, and we can see together how they have gussied it up." The fact that he asked me out for a Saturday night rather than a weekday reaffirmed my sense that something had shifted. This sounded very much like an official "date," and I was both thrilled and terribly nervous. All of those negative messages about my not being desirable, attractive, or womanly came back to haunt me, causing me to consult endlessly with friends about what I should wear and even, at one point, about whether I smelled okay. As a rule, I am not that concerned about clothes and have few doubts about my personal hygiene, but clearly I was extremely anxious. The actual date was much easier than the anticipation. We wandered around the Seaport, going in and out of Abercrombie and Fitch, Sharper Image, and other stores designed for the rich and famous, laughing at the thousand-dollar watch for the jogger and the outrageously expensive massage machines designed for every body part, at least those that were mentionable, which provoked us to conjure up massage gizmos for the unmentionable parts. "You have such beautiful brown eyes," Gene said, looking deeply into my eyes as we were finishing our meanderings, causing me to blush.

It was over dinner later that evening that Gene said, "I guess I owe you an explanation." As always, I feared a disability-related explanation about why things had moved so slowly between us, but in this case, I was totally off base. He explained that when we first met, he had just begun a relationship with another woman he had met through the *New York Review of Books*, and although he had been attracted to me on our first date, he was a strong believer in monogamy (for which I have always been grateful) and thus decided not to pursue our relationship any further. When he received my note a few months later, he remembered our pleasurable afternoon together and decided to see if we could at least become casual friends. By the end of the summer, his romance had ended, so when he got my postcard from New Mexico, he decided to give our relationship another try. Hence his Jewish New Year's card, which ultimately led to our peanut butter pie encounter.

Much later, Gene would insist that he told me on our first date that he was seeing someone. Doubtful, but what does it matter? We found each other in the end.

32. First Night

Soon after Gene and I began officially dating, he invited me to a holiday party at the home of one of his longtime friends. I was pleased that he wanted to introduce me to people who were important to him but also nervous about how they would react to me as a woman with a disability. As I've experienced so many times, people meeting me for the first time can have negative reactions, and I have never developed a thick-enough skin. After a lifetime of encounters with unwelcoming strangers, I tend to be shy and withdrawn in unfamiliar social scenes. I worried about how I would manage if Gene wandered off and left me to fend for myself. I had this stark memory of just such an occurrence when I was with Michael, my former fiancé. We went to a party hosted by one of his friends who had just received his Ph.D., and after Michael briefly introduced me around, I did not see him for the rest of the evening. I knew no one and spent most of the time parking myself on one or another of the various couches in the room, trying without much success to engage in conversation with whoever happened to sit down near me. At the end of the evening, when Michael came to collect me, he was surprised and annoyed that I had not had a good time.

I had never been in a group situation with Gene and wondered if I would have another evening of abandonment. As a sign of my anxiety, I got lost driving to Gene's house in Brooklyn Heights, where I was to pick him up so we could go to the party together, and had to call him from the middle of nowhere to confess that I didn't have a clue where I was. With much graciousness, he figured out a nearby landmark that I would be able to find, even in my lost state, Junior's Restaurant on Flatbush Avenue, and met me there. Then, as we were driving to his friend's house, apropos of nothing in our immediate conversation, he said something along the lines of "You know, you're going to this party with me, and we'll stay together all evening, so you don't have to worry about not knowing anyone." It was one of those beautiful, rare moments of feeling deeply understood and cared about by someone who at this stage did not know me all that well. True to his word, he never left my side the whole evening. He involved me in all his conversations with friends and told them enough about me to pique their interest in getting to know me. During the buffet dinner, potentially a nightmare for me given my difficulty balancing plates of food and liquids while milling and mingling, Gene asked how he could help and gave me exactly the help I needed, no more and no less. Gene was a true mensch that evening and a most caring one at that. While his friends at the party proved most welcoming, I have no doubt that Gene's warm, inclusive way of being with me set the tone.

That night Gene stayed over at my house, and we made love for the first time. This was another potentially anxious moment transformed into if not a passionate delight, then most definitely a tender, loving, at times humorous exploration between two bodies that barely knew each other, including one that had a predilection to do its own thing, regardless of the desires of its owner or her partner. The first challenge was for me to put in my diaphragm. I had thought that a diaphragm was an unlikely birth-control choice for a woman with cerebral palsy, particularly for one whose fingers wiggle and writhe, but a health practitioner at a local Planned Parenthood committed to serving people with disabilities convinced me that my left hand was coordinated enough to master the insertion of that rubbery ring, and after seemingly endless tries under her guidance and perseverance, some of which involved the diaphragm being flung from one end of the examining room to the other, I got the hang of it. However, my fingers were not nearly as cooperative when I knew Gene was eagerly awaiting my emergence from the bathroom. But finally success was mine, and I was both comforted and charmed by his honesty when he told me that I was not the first woman he had encountered who had had to do battle with her diaphragm.

After all these years, the specifics of how we proceeded from there escape me, and I'm not sure I would reveal them even if I could remember. What I recall most clearly was the simplicity,

clarity, and mutuality of our desire to connect in a deeply intimate, physical way, whatever that meant, however that happened,
and however much time we needed. And the sense that we didn't
have to learn everything or do everything all in one night, that
our sexual relationship was not going to be a one-night stand.

33. Mixed Couple

Disability is the difference that renders Gene and me a "mixed couple," and like any partners with a major difference in life experience or social status, we have had our issues. But, of course, no couple, no matter how similar the partners seem, avoids clashes and misunderstandings for long. As a friend and colleague who is a couples therapist once reminded me, intimate relationships are not for the fainthearted.

You Deceived Me

About three or four months after Gene and I had been together as a couple, I was invited to appear on a cable TV program to be shown on one of those public-access channels that most people don't watch. It was a "community issues" type show, and the theme for the episode was disabled women and girls, a topic I knew well. I agreed, feeling both pleased to be asked and horrified at the prospect of having to see myself on TV. This would be a hundred times worse than looking at myself in the mirror; there would be other viewers, although hopefully not that many, who would see and hear all the disability characteristics I found so disconcerting—my grimaces, my involuntary movements, my slurred speech. I also knew that these characteristics became more prominent when I was anxious, and there was no doubt that being on TV would make me nervous. The show was videotaped first and shown later. During the taping, each time the camera focused on me, I felt my face become contorted with anxiety. My sense of myself as freakish and unfeminine was very much with me.

A couple of weeks later, the show was aired, and Gene and I watched it together at his apartment. There was no question that my mouth and face were much more twisted and weird looking than they usually were when I was less stressed. I had seen myself like this several times before, so although I was quite unsettled by the image, I accepted that this was just one of those "anxiety" times and decided not to dwell on my appearance. Gene, on the other hand, had never seen my face so contorted; nor had he heard my speech quite so distorted. I didn't realize how disturbed he was until the conclusion of the program, when he blurted out, "I never realized you had so much involuntary movement." I interpreted his comment to mean that I was more disabled than I had originally appeared and that I had deceived him. "You know," I explained, "when I get very anxious, the muscles in my face get tighter, so I look weird and my speech is harder to understand. I don't like these changes either, but they don't mean I'm more disabled, just more anxious. I'm sorry that you got upset, but look at me now, sitting next to you. Do I look any different? I'm the same person I've always been." Gene could barely look at me; he became sullen and unresponsive.

Although I was distressed by his reaction and rejection, I surprised myself by not taking it personally. His negative response seemed to be more his problem than mine. This revelation was one of the many benefits of my involvement in the disability rights movement, where I had finally come to believe that negative attitudes, not my disability per se, were the real source of many of the problems I encountered out in the world. Gene, although highly knowledgeable about and deeply committed to challenging prejudice and discrimination of all types, was relatively new to disability rights; he was a quick study, but realistically, he could not have worked through the attitudes he had toward disability in a few short months. I understood this, but I didn't quite know what to do about the rejection I was experiencing at that moment. We had been planning to spend the night together, and although I was tempted to leave, I decided to stay, hoping that his continued contact with the real me might help counteract that disturbing image lingering in his mind. It was an unsuccessful strategy. We went through the motions of making love, but there was little pleasure or connection for either of us. When we left together in the morning, I had some difficulty opening the front door to his building, and he got angry, as though this difficulty was further confirmation of the limitations I had hidden from him. I was relieved to be able to leave and return to the safety of my own apartment.

That afternoon I flew off to New Orleans for a two-day business trip; we didn't speak before I left. While I was away, I kept hoping he'd call me at the hotel with words of conciliation, but I did not hear from him. I feared our relationship was over, and although I didn't feel responsible, I was despairing. Right before I left the hotel to come home, I called my answering machine; as a practicing psychotherapist, I should have called my machine every day to make sure that none of my patients were in crisis, but I hadn't, too caught up in my own crisis. I was thrilled to hear his voice on my machine. He explained that he had tried to call me at the hotel, but I had not been in my room, and he had been reluctant to leave a message with the desk for fear I would never get it. In the midst of a crisis, what message can you leave with a desk clerk? I do not remember more of what he said, except that somewhere he used the word "hon," and my mood instantly brightened. When I mentioned to my traveling companion how Gene's choice of words affected me, she understood but also joked, "Fifteen years into the women's movement and we're still seduced by words like 'hon' and 'babe.'" Maybe not seduced but definitely relieved.

Gene and I got together as soon as I got home. We were both nervous and a bit awkward, but his kiss at the door never tasted better. He said he had spent the past two days talking to some of his closest friends about why he had had such a strong reaction to seeing me on that cable show and what to do about it. They helped him think his feelings through, and he realized he owed me an apology. I felt at that moment extraordinarily lucky to have found a partner who was so clearly committed to grappling with problems related to my disability (or, as it would turn out, anything else that came between us) rather than denying or fleeing from them. I understood that his issues about my disability were not yet resolved. Why should they be when my own disability issues remained unresolved, even though at that point I'd been grappling with them for forty-plus years? But he was committed to working on them—and us. I couldn't ask for anything more, or better.

Advocacy Lessons for the Advocate

Over the years that Gene and I have been together, he has become increasingly knowledgeable about and committed to disability rights. He has readily engaged with and been embraced by my friends and colleagues from the movement, has joined me in protests, and has offered many insightful suggestions about how to infuse disability issues into leftist events and writings, which tend to overlook disability as a human rights issue. An avid newspaper reader, he is often ahead of me in tracking down the latest news and trends related to people with disabilities. Sometimes I have felt threatened by his disability-related knowledge and perceptiveness, as though I as the disabled member of the couple should be seen as the expert and deferred to, even when he is more knowledgeable or takes a different position on a disability issue. He has called me on my use of the disability card to silence him and/or win arguments on more than one occasion, and although I tend to bristle, he is often right.

One of Gene's closest friends founded an online journal for which he solicited contributions from diverse writers and activists. His policy was to never edit contributions, except when submissions contained overtly sexist, racist, homophobic, and other bigoted language, in which case he would ask for less offensive phrasing. After Gene and I were together for more than ten years, his friend received a submission for an upcoming journal issue that included the word *spastic* in a pejorative way. By definition, *spastic* refers to someone who has spasms; it is also a type of cerebral palsy that involves spastic muscles—my type of CP in fact. But *spastic* is often used in a derogatory way to describe someone who is clumsy, klutzy, awkward, and so forth, which was the way the word was used in the submission. This is one of many examples of how disability-related words are misappropriated to reflect negative characteristics in nondisabled people—for example, "Didn't you hear me? Are you deaf?" or "What's the matter with you? Are you a retard?" Such ableist language is pervasive yet often goes unchallenged, even by people who would not tolerate other forms of biased language. Gene read the piece before it went online and pointed out to his friend the inappropriate use of *spastic*, insisting that the word be changed. His friend did not agree with Gene's assessment and refused to ask the author to change the wording. Gene and his friend had a falling out over this, which resulted in their not speaking to each other for years.

I was shocked, not by the appearance of the word *spastic* but about the breakup in the friendship over it. I was accustomed to ableist language appearing in magazines written or edited by people whose non-disability-related politics I respected, and I tended to overlook their prejudiced choices. Actually, I was too complacent if not cowardly, particularly with the writing of people whom I liked and wanted to like me. I was a better advocate with strangers and acquaintances than with friends, whom I feared, if confronted, would abandon me. Gene was more courageous. In this case, he was being courageous on my issue, for me. I found that unbelievable. Was I really that important that he was willing to break up such a lengthy friendship? Impossible. So I rationalized away the cause of Gene's drastic action on my behalf. The misuse of *spastic* in the journal had not been the first source of disagreement between these two old friends; there had been considerable stress and strain in their relationship in recent years. I concluded that Gene had simply used his friend's rigidity over the use of that ableist term as an excuse to break off this increasingly difficult friendship. When I told him my assessment, he got angry and hurt, denying it was true. He was right, of course. Much later, I would apologize. What his friend had done was wrong, and he would not tolerate it. In love and politics, Gene is relentless in his commitments, bolstering my courage to be the same.

Difference, Not Defect

One evening, as I was finishing doing the dishes at Gene's apartment, he criticized me for failing to close the cap of the dishwashing detergent. Didn't I notice, he wondered, that he always kept the cap closed? I hadn't, but I would now. At first, his comments made me defensive. I was about to go on a rant: When he finishes doing the dishes at my place, he leaves the sponge full of soapy water, and hadn't he noticed that I prefer it to be squeezed dry; or when he folds the bath towel at my apartment, he folds it inside out with the label showing, and hadn't he noticed that I folded towels the other, "right" way? But then I stopped and laughed at myself. In so many ways, simple and complex, Gene and I are different. Some of the most profound knowledge I have gained during the years of our relationship is to hear and accept those differences, to not expect to change myself or him so that we "match," to not assume he thinks and feels like me or should.

My life's work has focused on acceptance and celebration of differences, yet for me personally, in my most intimate relationship, there remains a lingering fear that my differences reflect my defects. This is a residue of my early years of attempting to pass as nondisabled, as normal, well before I discovered that normalcy not only was overrated but didn't exist. Gene would ask me what movie I wanted to see, and I'd tried to second-guess what the right, normal answer would be—that is, what movie he wanted to see. That would distress him, not only because he would now have to second-guess my second-guess to try to figure out what movie I really and truly wanted to see but also because he was insulted by my underlying assumption that he was the normal member of the couple. He prided himself on keeping far away from every norm he could identify. Didn't I know that? "You're the one who grew up in a house, like most Americans. You're the one who owns a car. You're the one with money in the stock market. And you accuse *me* of being normal?" Gene has said in an exasperating tone on more than one occasion.

I've gotten better, but being honest has been risky. Speaking my mind, doing things my way can lead to disagreements, leaving the detergent bottle top open rather than closing it being the case in point, albeit a minor one. But it is often the minor disagreements that can lead to the biggest explosions. After all, dishes get washed several times a day, at least in my apartment, although not necessarily in Gene's, which is probably a good thing. At times, I have had to be determined and courageous not to interpret differences, especially those leading to disagreement, as a sign of my deficiency or defect. Oftentimes, a difference is just a difference, I've discovered to my surprise.

He doesn't think like me. I don't think like him. And these disparities are all okay. He cares whether the dishwashing detergent is closed, and I don't; he is oblivious to whether the towel labels show, and I'm not. There are differences between us, large and small. Of course, we also share a great deal in our political views, our mutual commitment to family and friends, our great sense of pleasure in hanging out on lazy Sunday afternoons with books, movies, and our favorite pussycat, Sylvester, and so much else. Those similarities can sometimes reinforce the notion that we are alike and I have thus achieved normalcy, until we do the dishes. Then I remember with pride that neither of us is normal.

34. Sylvester

Sunday ritual. Gene and I side by side in bed, a stack of DVDs at hand. As the movie marathon begins, Sylvester, Gene's big, boisterous tuxedo cat, stakes out his claim, leaping over Gene's body onto mine. He decides where to flop slowly, testing out my stomach, boobs, shoulders, and thighs for just the right combination of meat and bone. He sits, curls, or sprawls without regard to whether his tail is in my face or his claw in my rib. I am his chaise lounge, there for his comfort. His presence, his preference for my body, tickles me. It also terrifies me.

My body is in constant motion, especially when I'm lying down. I am at my own mercy, watching myself shake with no ability to stop it. Surely I could stop shaking if I really tried—a childhood myth perpetuated. My shame pervades. During sex I wonder how my lover will react. One is supposed to lose control through orgasm, not through a body wandering willy-nilly. My partner's reassurances are not convincing, a problem not unique to me or my palsied body.

As Sylvester lies on me in perfect stillness, dozing off, my shame impedes my pleasure. Will my movements shake him into wakefulness? Will I hurt him, pinching his tail now lodged between my thighs, or his pink nose snuggled between my knees? Will he abandon me for Gene's more dependable body? My fear intensifies the movements. I panic. Sylvester does not. My jerky movements cause him to shift his position ever so slightly and resume his sleep. When I pull away my leg, now cramping, he finds another available body part. There is little my body can do to dissuade him. Except sneezes, Gene's or mine. Those will send him off the bed, running for cover, only to return a few moments later to reclaim his chaise lounge.

Gene jokes that Sylvester always chooses me; his teasing is tinged with jealousy. He claims that Sylvester prefers my body precisely because of my movements, that he finds them soothing, like lying on a water bed. An intriguing notion, to be chosen for a bodily feature that has been a lifelong source of rejection. Sylvester will not confirm or deny the theory.

By picking me, whatever the cause, Sylvester has reduced my embarrassment about my body. Better than psychotherapy—cheaper, too. Maybe defects, differences don't matter all that much when it comes to being lovable. Maybe we can all be the cat's meow if we choose the right cat.

35. Faces of Eve

Sandy and I are dismantling our parents' house prior to selling it when we come upon old family photos in the attic. Three pictures jump out at me. Eve, my mother, looks like a flapper in this early photo, taken in 1930 when she was just twenty years old, sitting on the grass in a park with young people playing volleyball in the background, the hem of her blousy white dress up above her knees, her bobbed hair covered by a cute white cap, a string of shiny pearls around her neck. She looks content, without restraint, although already she has been restrained by a controlling, explosive older brother who chases away her beaus and steals her medal for being the fastest female runner in her school and by parents who insist that she go to work rather than college, despite her teachers' pleas. And she has begun to go out with my father, a quiet, sweet, exotic-looking man, a Sephardic Jew whose cultural restraints will prove the most restrictive of all, although she has yet to discover this. The picture suggests she could do anything, be anything, and that was my image of her throughout my childhood.

The wedding picture, the happy couple, 1934: My father in his black tux is outrageously handsome, like a movie star; my mother is her beautiful self but much more formal and subdued. She wears a long, white, semifitted gown covered in lace, with a floor-length veil attached to the back of her cap and swirled around her body, a bouquet of white orchids in her hand. The transformation from a flapper into a wife begins. She does not look unhappy but had not yet become aware of the calamity to hit the newlyweds soon after the honeymoon: the moving in of the difficult, controlling mother-in-law who does not speak English and looks down on my mother because she is an Ashkenazi Jew, a "Yiddisha" (Ashkenazim traditionally speak Yiddish) rather than the Sephardic, Ladino-speaking girl that this old-world matriarch expected each of her four sons to marry. The plan had been for this meddlesome mother to live with an older son, as was tradition. However, this wise elder son, or more to the point, his new wife, rejected her at the last moment, and my compliant father conceded to take her in. My mother will be tormented for years until she threatens to leave my father, their firstborn child, Eli, in hand, if he does not oust his mother and move away from East New York, Brooklyn, where his relatives live, to Bensonhurst, Brooklyn, where my mother's family resides. My father concedes again, this time to his wife—to my sister's and my good fortune.

The final photo: my mother, Eli, Sandy, and Sandy's adult daughter Linda standing in a lineup pose with Mayor Koch smack in the middle; where else would His Honor be? The picture was taken in 1989 at my swearing-in ceremony to become one of the New York City Commissioners on Human Rights, a position conferred as the result of my advocacy work on behalf of women and girls with disabilities. My mother, then close to eighty, looks a bit worn out but happy, a big smile on her face and a camera in her hand. She appears a proud mother, with no sign of ambivalence about her younger daughter's achievement. Yet, when I and my fellow commissioners are asked to stand and raise our right hand to take the oath of office, my mother, seated in the audience, instinctively stands, saying the oath aloud, as though she were me, our boundaries crossed and lost, until my father and Eli gently pull her down. Eli would later describe the scene he encountered that morning: "When I went to pick up Mom and Dad, Mom refused to get out of bed. She seemed out of it, muttering something I couldn't make out, one minute angry, the next minute crying. I thought we'd have to leave her home, but Dad and I finally coaxed her out of bed, walked her around a bit, and then she seemed fine. Maybe she had a mini-stroke." My dad and Sandy tentatively agreed with that diagnosis. I wondered if the culprit was also jealousy and grief for the life she might have had had she not been unduly restricted. For her, as for so many other women, marriage had not been the fairy-tale dream that I had longed for and feared was not open to me when I was a young girl with a disability. Unexpectedly, having a disability increased rather than decreased my options as a woman—to study, to work, to explore my identity, to become an activist, to paint, to write, and then to find my true love, when I knew who I was (more or less).

The next five years until her death were filled with bouts of anger, much of it directed at my quiet, sweet father, who without conscious awareness or malicious intent had honored the Sephardic tradition of male dominance during their fifty years of marriage, unilaterally making their major life decisions. Her desire to go back to work after the children were school-age or even out of the house? No, a working wife would reflect badly on my father's ability to provide. Colorful evening gowns? No, they undermine the principles of modesty and refined taste. Travel adventures after my father retired? No, there's no place like home. A cute red sports car for my mother? No, too gaudy. Eve ultimately did get her flashy red car by threatening divorce, only half in jest, but within a year or two she became too physically weak and mentally confused to drive. How I wish I had a picture of her racing that jazzy buggy. The flapper returns.

36. Tough Bird

My father is dying, or at least he is retreating very deeply inside himself, perhaps never to reemerge as his old self. Even as his old self, he was quite retiring—in stark contrast to my lively, feisty, in-your-face mother—but as he himself acknowledged, that was part of the attraction, or at least his attraction to her. So now he has become even more silent than his usual silent self. I have always been more like him than my mother, in looks as well as in temperament. We would sometimes sit together in a room like a pair of bookends, encompassing voluminous space between us, but it was space filled with unspoken stories and mutual understanding. Now as I sit with him, the space feels empty, and I have already abandoned my meager efforts to fill it up with words that he seems not to attend to or understand. Yet it is still comforting to sit next to him in his hospital room and hold his hand, when he lets me, or hope for some glimmer of recognition in his eyes, when I can coax them open. I take solace in the fact that he still looks like my father. More than two months of hospitalization with pneumonia and his necessary abandonment of eating for a feeding tube have not detracted from his good looks: white, silky hair characteristic of him since his thirties, dark complexion and eyes like mine—or rather, I should say mine like his—and a combination of features that have always made him distinguished looking, like an ambassador. He looks the same, yet there appears to be nobody home behind his forehead; my sister and I prefer to think that he has simply removed himself to another, more distant place, one that I hope is more pleasurable than the bleak confines of this hospital room. Perhaps he is readying himself to leave for a more permanent home, a thought that for me is both frightening and reassuring. I suspect that my mother, who died several years previously, is not yet ready to receive him, so he may have to bide his time a bit longer. My mother always loved traveling, while my dad is a homebody. My fantasy about her after her death was that she had hooked up with one of her deceased sisters or best friends and together they were traveling through the fifty states, one of her dreams. She has probably not had quite enough time to hit all fifty just yet; she may be milking a cow on some farm in Iowa as I write this. But sooner or later she will be done, or she may have to cut short her meandering to welcome my father, repeating in death a pattern that was so confining for her in life. I'd like to think, though, that this time she wouldn't concede her freedom so readily. I have no doubt that for a few days he can manage on his own.

I can focus on my mother with much greater ease. She was the free spirit that I wished I could be, so I am always eager to glorify her. My father is far more restrained and restricted in ways that are too familiar. Yet by his standards, and even mine, he had a very expansive life. At age twelve, he and his mother, brothers, and sister had come to the Lower East Side in New York City from Monastir, a town in the Balkans. The family was extremely poor; my father started his work life shining shoes on a street corner, getting up at three o'clock in the morning to secure a prime spot for passersby. He ultimately lived the American dream by establishing his own women's sportswear company and making far more money than he ever imagined possible, able to afford houses and cars and his children's education and to give back to the Sephardic community in ways that made him proud. As his daughter, I see him having few unrealized dreams. Sadly, he also has little awareness of the ways that he and his male-dominated culture oppressed my mother, leaving her with a lifetime of unfulfilled fantasies that increasingly ate away at her, as she got older and was no longer able to be in perpetual motion, no longer able to run away from her disappointments and her fury. To me, my mother's death seemed like a welcome respite from her heartbreak and rage. Yet I envision my father's death, when it comes, more as a sense of closure on a fulfilled life.

None of this should be interpreted to mean that I am ready to let him go. I want to linger with him a bit longer, to do I'm not sure what. Make sense of the relationship or perhaps just avoid becoming an orphan.

I have this panicky feeling inside me, like I am on the verge of tears or hysteria or both. My father's critical condition is wearing me down. Seeking respite through my avocation as a visual artist, I try to do some painting on a new project. I have taken a large sheet of watercolor paper and drawn a set of horizontal and vertical lines that create a set of small square boxes or cells. I hope to use the cells as a visual daily diary, creating a different image with a different medium each day, or for as many days as I can manage. Today I face sixteen empty cells, a blank sheet. I decide to initiate the first cell, hoping that will set me into a pattern of daily work and, with that cell, take what I think will be the path of least resistance—using mess-free colored markers and drawing birds, one of my favorite subjects. But my anxiety begins rising as soon as the pen hits the paper, an overwhelming sense of self-judgment that every stroke is the wrong one. Although the room is fairly cool, I break out in a sweat, and I begin dropping pens as though they are hot potatoes. My impulse is to quit, partly because a bad first picture will discourage me from taking up the pen or brush tomorrow. Yet part of me knows my intense fear of failure has little to do with the quality of the painting I am creating. My father is failing, and I am, too, in empathy, in fear, in helplessness. But he's a tough bird. He didn't die last Thursday night when Sandy and I spent all night with him in close vigil, wanting to make sure he did not die alone. Despite his labored breathing and dropping blood pressure, the ton of antibiotics pumped into him did their magic, and he was alert the next morning, mumbling to me, I'm quite sure, "Take me home!" And who could blame him for that request? The doctor was astounded. So in honor of that tough bird, I give birth to a couple of my own birds on that blank sheet of paper. They are not perfect, but then again, neither was he, although I'd have to say by most measures he has been an exceptionally caring father.

The birds on the page prove less interesting, at least to me, than the background, a set of multicolored lines and dots that have the quality of a spider's web or a fisherman's net, perhaps an attempt to hold on to the birds a bit longer than might be my due. The hundred colored pens drop to the floor as soon as I complete my task, as though my inner chaos needs to remind me of its presence, refusing to be calmed by the pretty picture. I pick up the pens in a state of fury, only to drop them all again after I had secured them in their orderly place in the box. I am tempted to leave them lying on the floor, but I am most intolerant of external mess when that too closely mirrors my internal experience. This time, though, I make little effort to organize the pens by color as I return them to their box, as though some disorder might inspire me to pick up the pens more readily next time.

37. Hand in Hand

From the time that my father visibly began aging—in his mid-eighties—until his death, an important aspect of our relationship was sitting together in front of the television holding hands. His limited hearing and erratic memory made more than the briefest of conversations almost impossible. He became increasingly withdrawn and unreachable, particularly after my mother died, six years before his death. My taking his hand and massaging his fingers restored the connection and enabled me to literally and figuratively hold on to the man who had been one of my staunchest supporters through much of my life and who was now preparing to leave me.

These hand-holding encounters seemed meager in comparison to the extensive amounts of concrete caregiving provided by Sandy and the Jamaican home health aide that we had hired together. After my mother died, Sandy had abandoned her own home to live with my father, who we knew could not survive alone. She had forsaken much of her own life several years earlier to care for my dying mother. After both my parents were gone, we calculated that she had given up a decade of her life to focus on their care.

Then again, caregiving was a primary part of her identity, well before my parents began declining. Internalizing the expectations for women of her generation—she grew up in the 1950s—she saw herself primarily as a wife, mother, and, more broadly, caregiver of anyone and everyone who needed help. In contrast, I, as a woman with a disability, was socialized to believe that I couldn't and shouldn't be a caregiver, that I was more likely to need rather than provide help. The incompleteness of my socialization was perhaps suggested by the fact that I did choose a career that involved caregiving—I became a social worker and psychotherapist—and while there were many reasons for that career choice, I could not deny that one aspect was to feel more womanly through caregiving. In an odd twist, my involvement in the women's movement led me to make that choice. In a women's consciousness-raising group, I discovered my own dormant caregiving capacities and decided to nurture them.

Experiencing the decline of first my mother and then my dad reactivated my early self-doubts about caregiving. There was a piece of reality here. There were aspects of physical caretaking that were in fact problematic for me to undertake, like feeding and lifting, given the involuntary movements in my arms and hands and my uneven gait. But some of my doubts were really old ghosts revived by the stress of my parents' deterioration. I was quick to defer to my sister's judgments on caregiving issues, even when I thought my judgments might be sounder than hers. Guilt and gratitude compounded the picture; she was, after all, sacrificing her life, while I was more or less living mine. However, at some point my caregiving knowledge as a disability activist, feminist, therapist, and sane person kicked in, and the balance of power shifted somewhat, although we never achieved full equity. I did, for example, help her challenge her superwoman notion of herself, encouraging her to consult with doctors when my father showed new symptoms rather than accepting her belief that she did or should know best. And I was able to intervene when she came into conflict with my father's home health aide, who lived with her in my father's house and was equally strong-willed. As a disabled woman, I understood the oppression that the aide experienced as a woman of color, who despite her many capacities had limited access to resources and hence was stuck in a low-paying job. However, lucky for us, she was exceptionally fond of my dad and eager to give him the best care. When her definition of "best care" didn't agree with Sandy's or mine, I was willing to cut her some slack, not to patronize her, since I hate people patronizing me or anyone else, but to be open to the possibility that she might have a better take on a situation than Sandy or I did. When there were conflicts over money, I was her staunch advocate, appalled at the low wages that home health aides receive, which to me reflected bias based on gender, race, and class.

There was also the whole issue of pacing and taking care of oneself during times of stress, which Sandy, like many female caregivers, tended to overlook. Her typical pattern was to provide care nonstop for too long, burn herself out, and then flee for what were at times lengthy and unpredictable periods, creating great stress on my father and his backup caretakers. I would periodically send her off against her will or simply give her permission to claim bits and pieces of her own life totally apart from the caregiver role. In truth, I was as much a caregiver to the caregiver as to the parent in need of care.

I began to realize as I sat week after week, and then, as his situation deteriorated, day after day, holding my father's hand, that I didn't need to devalue my role as caregiver. I was, in effect, caring about him and facilitating his care even if I wasn't literally giving him all the concrete care he needed. And hand-holding can serve so many functions. It was for him both a barometer to the world (my cold hand meant that it was winter) and a measure of my well-being, which he never stopped caring about (my unduly slender hand meant that I was too stressed to eat). And perhaps most important, our holding hands was a key to locked-up memories about his very long, full, rich life. My hand triggered his stories about hand-holding with my mother—their secret dates and grasping each other's hands under the table at the Fulton Fish Market in lower Manhattan for years before they were allowed to marry—and with his mother, a widow who came to Ellis Island in 1919 with several young children in hand, including my father. After my father passed away, I experienced many senses of loss but perhaps none so visceral as not being able to ever again hold his hand.

V

Why Claim Disability?

38. Finding My Way

It is a few days since I have arrived in this lush city in South America to attend a working conference on violence against women, bringing together twenty community leaders from Latin America, the United States, and Canada. The goal is to build an inter-American network, but the conference is poorly designed, with too much emphasis on "talking heads" and not enough on dialogue and informal networking. As the only disabled woman there, I face the usual barrier of being seen as an unwelcome outsider to a group of women who are trying to be respectful of cultural differences but draw the line at disability. Disability is seen as deficiency rather than difference, with no redeeming qualities; at best, it evokes guilt, since few around the table have made an attempt to include disabled women in their work, although when challenged, they agree they should, or at least somebody should. They appear unable or unwilling to conceive of the possibility that disability could be a source of strength and culture, that inclusion could strengthen, not burden, their programs. Cut off midstream because of time restrictions, my presentation, limited to statistics on the high rates of abuse of women and girls with disabilities, reinforces the notion of disabled women as victims rather than survivors and advocates. As a talking head with slow, halting speech patterns and unfamiliar body movements, my very presence further confirms their stereotypes about what it means to be disabled and female—sick, dependent, incompetent, vulnerable. Yet the fact that I am at the table as a peer rather than across the table as a client simultaneously challenges their negative assumptions. During the Q&A period, no questions are directed at me, although at the break, a woman approaches me with tears in her eyes: "You don't know how much it meant to me to hear you" ("and to see you," I imagine her thinking, "out of the institution where you belong"). Such emotional responses are typical in my life as a public speaker and are the clearest evidence of my failure to take listeners to a new level of awareness about disability and the lives of disabled women. There is little about my life that merits crying, other than my constant exposure to people who insist on crying about me; they infuriate me more than those who are overtly hostile. I feel most tempted to scream at, if not smack, the criers. But I remain a well-adjusted crippled girl and accept the woman's comments with as much graciousness as I can muster. I tell myself that being cried at is better than being rendered invisible, although I am not entirely convinced.

Later on in the conference I talk with a few participants who have done a bit of work on disabled women or are making some convincing noises to the effect that they'd like to. Their comments help move me off of my island, that isolated, I'm-the-only-one space that I am quick to retreat to when I am not readily welcomed by a new group of nondisabled people. That island is an easy answer for me, one that has become part of my identity after years of exclusion; it is familiar, if not necessarily comfortable, and hence hard to give up. To attempt to push my way in rather than passively withdraw always feels riskier. My rational self knows that there are other participants at this conference who feel a similar isolation for different reasons, such as race or income level, yet don't retreat quite so quickly.

By the end of the conference I've built a few bridges, albeit unsteady ones that need further reinforcement to hold. And I remember what I know but usually resist and resent, which is that I am inevitably seen as a freak or "the other" at first but that time is on my side. As hours, and preferably days, pass, I begin to blend in with others and slowly shift from the periphery to a place slightly closer to the center. The shift has its advantages—at the very least, there's company for dinner—but it also comes with a price, sometimes too dear to pay. With those women uncomfortable with disability, I need to be cautious, to avoid appearing too different, too weird, so that I am not exiled once more. The island, however, the place in my head where I retreat in the face of real or anticipated rejections and say what I really know and feel, tolerates my most outrageous self who flaunts her differences with pride and fights exclusion without apology.

39. Keeping the Distance

During my reading at a women's studies class—an effort by the professor, a dear friend of mine, to infuse disability into the curriculum—I look up to see one of the students, a young woman, crying. I have been telling a tale about my mother teaching me to drive. My mother's persistence and insistence despite my resistance make everyone laugh except this student. My mind is flooded with questions:

What do you see or hear that transforms a typical mother-daughter tangle into a tragedy? Surely you, barely twenty, still struggling to escape your own mother's grasp, know all about the maneuvering and machinations of mothers and their defiant, at times desperate, daughters.

Have you pushed me away, turned me into an outsider? The crippled girl's triumph over adversity, driving despite her disability? Or is it the presence of the crippled girl herself, her odd movements and halting voice, that evokes your tears, overpowering the meaning of her words?

How can I convince you that the tragedies of my life have to do with commonplace disappointments, disillusionments, and losses—the lover, the job that got away, the death of someone dear—not disability? Perhaps I can't. You need to keep me at a distance, as though I were contagious. To see me as a sister scares you, shakes you, shocks you. Then I would be like you, and what's worse, you would be like me. Better you should see me as courageous.

It makes me cry.

40. That "Inspirational" Label

It's better than nothing, that "inspirational" word that flows off your tongue like a bribe. Better than being rendered invisible, not seen at all, I suppose. Better than having you cross the street to avoid me, as though I were an eyesore, a disgusting thing that you can't bear to look at. Frankly, I'd rather you wait until you get past your initial, superficial, prejudicial reactions, see who I am, and then decide if you like me or even hate me—at least those judgments would be real.

41. Token of Approval

I was a feminist before I was a disability activist. In the early 1970s, I joined a women's consciousness-raising group, where I discovered my commonalities with other women. I was amazed to find out that the other women in the group hated parts of their bodies and doubted their womanliness like I did. Together we learned that our self-doubts were grounded in society's sexist attitudes, not in our personal defects, enabling us to develop a political consciousness and claim our own strengths. Through that group I found a sense of community after a lifetime of being an outsider; my disability was not a barrier to sisterhood. When I became a disability activist in the late 1970s, I was eager to bring my disability consciousness into the women's movement, expecting feminists to welcome me and my disabled sisters as I had been welcomed by that group.

At first, there was no welcome mat; rather, the entry door was slammed shut. Women's conferences were held in inaccessible locations, and conference organizers showed little interest in including issues of disabled women on the program. But gradually, conference sites became more accessible, and one or two workshops on disabled women began appearing. I led some of those early workshops, only to discover that few if any nondisabled feminists attended them. By the late 1980s, disabled women were invited to present at workshops on not only disability but also mainstream women's issues, such as salary inequities in the workplace and sexual harassment, and occasionally they were invited to give keynote speeches. As a result, more and more nondisabled feminists began to hear about disability issues, whether they wanted to or not.

But they still didn't quite get what we were saying. Many of the responses to our presentations were of the "You're so inspirational" variety. We rarely got invitations to join in informal activities during the conference, such as evening networking sessions at the hotel bar, or to sit on conference planning committees, much less on the governing boards of the women's organizations spearheading these conferences. I was deeply disturbed and perplexed by the distance that I felt from the women's community. Feminists understood oppression based on sexism. And they seemed to understand the multiple forms of bias that African American women, poor women, lesbians, and other "minority" groups of women faced (although I would later discover that their understanding of these groups was less comprehensive than I had thought and that what they had learned was only in response to pressure from these groups). Why didn't they grasp the double whammy of sexism and disability bias? Why were they reacting to me and other disabled women in the same negative ways as the politically unsophisticated world did?

So I had not expected that phone call in the spring of 1992. "Would you like to join our board of directors?" Claudia asked. Claudia was the executive director of a prominent women's fund in the Midwest—one of the first of many throughout the country that had been established specifically to fund projects by and for women and girls. After immediately answering, "Yes," I thought, "Ah, disabled women have finally arrived in the women's movement." "You won't have an easy job," she went on to say. "You'll be the first disabled woman on the board. Our fund has become wonderfully diverse in recent years. But when it comes to disabled women . . . Well, for us, that's been the last and hardest group to include." "Don't worry," I said assuredly. "We'll figure out together how to do it."

I had met Claudia at a human rights conference in which one of the speakers made some sexist comments and we both went at him. We immediately bonded, and over lunch she mentioned a small research project her fund was undertaking on how young women in their twenties make career choices. I explained to her that the issue for disabled women was not so much what type of work they would choose but whether they would be able to work at all given the barriers they faced. Claudia seemed very interested. "You know," she said somewhat apologetically, "we haven't included any disabled women in the study so far. We have so little money for the study." I wasn't going to let lack of funds stop her, so I offered to convene a group of my disabled women friends for a conference call with her researcher. She was delighted with the offer.

On the conference call, as my friends and I exchanged experiences, the fund's researcher took copious notes, which she incorporated into her report. When the report was published, I had every disabled woman activist I know call Claudia to thank her for being inclusive. A few months later, she was on the phone inviting me to join the board.

And so began a very ambivalent six-year period in my life. I had high hopes of transforming the organization into one that was totally inclusive of disabled women's issues in every aspect of its work. Such naïveté. Such unrealistic expectations, given my previous years of frustration with the women's movement. I did some good while I was there, such as facilitating the funding of some projects for disabled women and girls. And I personally benefited by meeting some extraordinary women on the board who facilitated my career as an activist and an artist. A few, by sharing their personal, often limited resources to help other women move forward, were good role models and inspired me to do the same.

In hindsight, perhaps the greatest benefit to me (although it did not feel like a benefit at the time) was an up-close and personal glimpse into the way that women's and other organizations—and political movements—change to become more inclusive of any group: slowly and with difficulty, if at all.

I remember in great detail that first board meeting. Famous feminists whom I was accustomed to seeing on TV or conference podiums were now sitting across the table. They were warm and welcoming, even when I spilled an entire cup of coffee while carrying it from the buffet to my seat. After that incident I had many people volunteering to carry for me anything and everything. There were several other new board members, women representing various racial and ethnic groups, at that meeting, so the first order of business was to fill us in on the fund's history, mission, goals, and programs. When we were handed the mission statement, which included a commitment to address and redress the various types of bias that women face, I hit the first speed bump. The more than twenty million women with disabilities in America had not yet shown up on the fund's radar screen. I immediately drew their attention to this serious omission. Claudia and some of the old-timers on the board appeared somewhat embarrassed, and fairly quickly the board voted to amend the mission statement to include disability bias. That was a victory, one that my disabled sisters around the country immediately appreciated. But as I would discover, mission statements, like laws, were not always enforced.

We next reviewed the docket of grant proposals under consideration for funding. The board's job was to vote on the projects after the staff had carefully screened and approved the proposals. We were not a rubber stamp; we rejected some proposals that the staff had accepted. I have to confess to enjoying a heady sense of power. After applying for so many grants and feeling at the mercy of funders, I was gratified to be on the other side, to be a decision maker for a change. But even stronger than the feeling of power was my fascination with the kinds of programs and projects women's groups were developing. They gave me ideas about programs that might benefit disabled women.

But why weren't there programs for disabled women of any type already on the grants docket? Claudia explained that they simply didn't receive many proposals involving disabled women, maybe one or two a year, and that this quarter they had received none. I wasn't completely surprised. Given the architectural, transportation, communication, financial, and other barriers that disabled women faced, many had a hard enough time getting out into the community to do the basics of daily life much less to develop programs. Nonetheless, I knew there were at least a number of disabled women's projects around the country, so there should have been more proposals than Claudia described. I offered to beat the bushes to get more proposal submissions; Claudia and the board were appreciative.

I didn't negotiate the board's postmeeting ritual nearly as smoothly. It was customary after meetings for everyone to dine together and, after dinner, to engage in group discussions of a personal, if not intimate, nature, greatly facilitated by a few glasses of wine. For me, that discussion was initiation by fire. "So what was your wildest, weirdest sexual encounter during adolescence?" was the topic that emerged that night. I found myself thinking, "Can we get back to talking about program proposals? Please!" Having had an asexual adolescence, I knew I was in big trouble. I initially decided to concoct a story, but as I heard some of the other women's outrageous accounts of sexual acts I had never conceived of, I knew my imagination was not up to the task. "I was a virginal good girl," I confessed when my turn came. Then, when the laughter died down, I heard "Me, too" emerge from the mouth of another board member. "Me three," said yet another. "Well, my dears," said one of the women who had told a particularly lewd story, "You three are entitled to a totally risqué middle age. Don't let the rest of us down. We expect to hear stories. And soon!" I could see I was going to learn more from my sisters on the board than I had realized.

Between meetings I networked with as many disabled women as I could, encouraging them to submit proposals to the fund. At the next meeting the head of development proudly showed me the invitation for the fund-raising event that the entire board was scheduled to attend that night after the meeting. She wanted to make sure I had noticed the disability access symbol, the by-now-familiar small, stylized image of a wheelchair, on the lower corner of the invitation. She explained that Claudia and the staff had decided that from now on, all of the fund's events would be held in accessible sites, and all notices about events would bear the access symbol. I thanked her but was less ecstatic and effusive than she might have expected. By then I had already encountered too many women's organizations that demonstrated their commitment to disabled women by providing ramps and sign-language interpreters at their programs—and not doing anything else. By 1993 we should have gone beyond the realm of symbolism. I was waiting to see some substance.

Sure enough, on the docket of potential grants there were still no proposals focused on disabled women. The fund had, in fact, received two related to disability, but, I was told, neither was quite right: One was in too early a stage of development; the other was in a topic area not typically covered by the fund. "Maybe we need to be a bit more creative or flexible if we want to support disabled women's projects," I said to Claudia and the rest of the board. "Perhaps we need to give some planning or start-up grants. Or consider supporting projects even if they are not exactly in the areas we typically fund." "Maybe," Claudia said. "But you know, we have such a limited grant-making budget. I'd hate to dilute our focus. We can't bend over backward to meet the needs of every group." But they already had "bent over backward" for groups of women that they considered "priorities," including women of color and poor women. Of course, racism and poverty had severe consequences for women, but I could never quite make sense of this notion of the hierarchy of oppressions. How can we say that one group of oppressed women has suffered more than another? Besides, what about disabled women of color or, better yet, poor disabled women of color (a group I knew well from my work with the mentoring project for disabled girls)? Where do they fit in? But I held my tongue and my questions. I was still learning the ropes and trying to find my place. I didn't want to make trouble.

And then the conversation shifted. "So what type of gown is everyone wearing to tonight's fund-raising event?" one of the longtime board members asked. "Gowns?" I had thought that my simple black cocktail dress would do. Even that was a stretch for me. I had given up wearing dresses or even skirts some time ago. "And just how feminist is it to be comparing gowns?" I wondered. Quite feminist, I discovered, as each of the strong, powerful, politically savvy women sitting around the table began to describe in great detail the gown she was planning to wear. I had to tell them that I had misjudged the dress code and had brought from home, several hundred miles away, only a plain black sheath. "Not to worry," said one of the women. I have a fabulous gown you can borrow; it's just your size." "And if that doesn't work," said another woman, "there's a darling dress shop right around the corner from here. I'll help you pick something that's just right." It was my first experience with feminists as fashionistas. Live and learn.

The fund-raising event itself was a who's who of feminism, including founders of some of the other women's funds and, of course, a lot of very wealthy women (and men). Claudia made it a point to introduce me to everyone who was anyone. Maybe she was eager to show off her token "crip," but frankly, I didn't care. I kept thinking, "If I make a few or even one of these big-shot people aware of the issues of disabled women, that will be an achievement." I was hopeful that some of the contacts I made at this event would lead to opportunities to promote my work and, to be honest, myself. I wasn't disappointed. People that I met at this fund-raising event and others would lead to a host of speaking engagements, invitations to join the board of directors of other women's organizations, some honors for my work, and even the sale of a few of my paintings.

Ego stroking aside, with each successive board meeting, I was seeing little evidence of disabled women benefiting from my participation on the board. "So what's the story?" my disabled women friends would ask. "Any more dollars from that fund of yours going to disabled women?" "No," I had to confess. "They're not receiving too many proposals from disabled women." "Oh, please. I'll bet that's just the kind of excuse they used to use to keep out African American women from knocking on their door," said one of my more outspoken friends. "Oh, no," I said. "Women of color have a great deal of power in that fund." "And how about ten years ago? Or even five? Did they have power then, or were they tokens like you?" she asked. I didn't know, but of course she was right. The fund had been started by white, middle-class women, as had the larger women's movement. Women of color had to scream, yell, pressure, threaten, boycott, and fight their way into both the fund and the movement to lessen if not fully overcome the racism they encountered. Other minorities didn't have a much easier time. A chance encounter a few years into my tenure on the board told the tale. I met a Native American woman and a Latina who had joined the board when I had, but each had dropped out within the first year, claiming too many other responsibilities. But they both told me they had left because they found the fund unresponsive to their community's needs. And later on, after I had left the organization, I met a woman who was one of "the first and only" African American women on the board. She, too, had departed early and could barely describe her experiences without becoming enraged.

I regret that I hadn't paid closer attention to my friend's comment—or hadn't met those women earlier. Then I might have

seen the resistance to including disabled women that I was beginning to encounter in a larger context of the organization's resistance to change.

The fund continued to receive few if any proposals involving
disabled women that fit its criteria, and I didn't push the plan-
ning/start-up grant suggestion. Without Claudia's support, I
didn't think that idea would stand a chance. I do believe that if
there had been a will, that group of women on the board would
have found a way. For example, they could have mandated that
all community groups receiving funds must make an effort to include disabled women in their projects. Or they could have provided a financial incentive, maybe a few thousand dollars extra, to
groups that included disabled women in their programs.

Eventually, by pushing and shoving, I got a few results for my
efforts. For example, a special initiative to promote the career development of young women included a project for disabled women
that got a fair amount of press. But there were not nearly enough
grants to show a strong, clear commitment to disabled women.

The funding of projects with specific disability content wasn't
the only way the fund fell short. The presence of disabled women
in programs designed to raise awareness of general women's issues
was, from my perspective, limited. For example, there was a big
"women's right to choose" campaign that included a survey of
women's attitudes and a blitz in the media. I encouraged the inclusion of disabled women in the survey, reminding Claudia that
they might have some different attitudes toward choice than nondisabled women, particularly regarding when and how disability
is used to justify abortion. "We already know about the attitudes
of disabled women," Claudia told me. And I suppose she did, because unlike some other media campaigns on choice that I had
seen, there was nothing in the materials about aborting disabled
fetuses. But I would have preferred to have the voices of disabled
women included in a more direct way. Also, in a poster promoting
the fund's young women's career project that included images of a
diverse group of young women, there were no women with visible
disabilities. When I expressed my concern to one of the department heads of the fund, who was Latina, she said, "Well, there are
no Latina women portrayed in the poster either." And I thought

to myself, "Just because you are a poor advocate for your community, I should be one too?"

Increasingly over time, I felt like a one-song Suzie, constantly repeating the question, "What about disabled women?" I grew to hate my own ineffective voice among these women, raging at myself as much as at them. I kept thinking if only I were a better activist, if only I screamed louder, if only I weren't so eager to fit in, if only I were a better conversationalist and could sweet-talk some of the other board members into supporting my issue, if only, if only. Not all my rants against myself were unwarranted. I was not the ideal "first and only" disabled woman for this organization. I was not willing enough to go out on a limb for what I believed in and run the risk of being rejected by this group of feminists that I was so eager to be part of. Although I had been "out of the closet" as disabled for more than fifteen years, I was still a bifurcated woman, struggling between and straddling the disabled and nondisabled worlds. I wanted to belong somewhere but wasn't at home anywhere. I was afraid to make waves, ambivalent about power, and hence too often kept quiet to keep the peace, to find my place at the table. In fact, part of the problem was that I was trying to create change by myself, a Lone Ranger who really needed to be part of a posse.

In the midst of my disillusionment, Claudia began moving the fund in a new direction. Thanks to a huge donation from a private donor, she was transforming the organization into a much larger, stronger, and more powerful resource, voice, and presence for women. The move would have a price, one that made my goal of including disabled women even more difficult to achieve. The transformation started with a change in board functions. The board would no longer review and approve grants but would focus instead on "higher-level" tasks like setting overall fund policies and building a substantial endowment. Claudia must have known that I would be upset by the board's loss of its right to review the grants docket because she called me before the meeting to let me know that a vote on this issue was on the agenda. Of course, I was upset. This was the only modicum of control I had over the fund's grant making with regard to disabled women, paltry though it was. I voted no at the meeting, but most of the rest of the board voted yes, so I was overruled. Later on, a few other board members said they wanted to vote no also but felt it was pointless. They knew Claudia would ultimately have her way.

The new emphasis on fund-raising finally led me to leave before the end of my second term. Requiring board members to raise money was not unique to this women's fund; it became increasingly common among most women's organizations. While I understood that this was essential for survival, I was disturbed by its effects on the board and the organization. "We need to invite some women of wealth—or at least women who know some women of wealth—to join our board," Claudia had remarked. "I thought board members are supposed to represent the diverse communities of women that our fund serves," one of my sister board members responded. "We know enough about diversity. Now we need money," Claudia explained. And at that moment, I felt corporate America descending on us. Over time, we did have increasing numbers of women of wealth and women who held prominent positions in large corporations join our board or in other ways become involved with the fund, in some ways shifting it in a more conservative direction. I felt increasingly impotent since I was by no means a woman of wealth, had no connections to wealthy people, and represented a constituency of women who were among the poorest of the poor and hence were not potential donors.

After I quit the board, I became temporarily preoccupied with my lack of effectiveness. I felt that, overall, I hadn't done much for the fund—a few grants here, a few programs there; mainly I felt like a thorn in the fund's, and particularly the executive director's, side. But as other women who had been through similar experiences would later reassure me, the first and only of any group who joins a mainstream organization never does much. My presence was just a beginning, a baby step. I don't regret the six years I spent there. I learned a great deal about the slow pace of progress and the need for patience, perseverance, and most important, realistic expectations.

Being on that board also gave me a higher level of credibility in the women's community. Now I was associated with not only a mentoring project for disabled adolescent girls but also a well-known, highly respected women's fund. The connection with that fund led to invitations to join the boards of other women's organizations, also as the first and only disabled woman. "What? Again? Didn't I learn from experience?" I would ask myself each time I accepted another invitation. Actually, I did. While I didn't have a major impact on any of these organizations, I was less frustrated and depressed because I didn't expect to make a big dent. By then, I was pleased to have any impact, even if all I did was open the door a bit. There were some considerable achievements: a number of grants for disabled women's projects from the second women's fund I joined; a heightened awareness of accessibility when another women's group whose board I served on was purchasing a new building; and, one of my most exciting moments, a congressional hearing on the issues of young disabled women, orchestrated by a third group. I have to acknowledge that those hearings were not my idea. They were the brainchild of the president, who had been advocating for the rights of disabled women, not exclusively, but as part of her work on behalf of all women, for more years than I had, even though she had never before invited a disabled woman to join her board. My presence on the board served as a catalyst to further her work on behalf of disabled women and girls, but I didn't have to do much advocacy. My tenure on that board demonstrated how much easier it is to promote inclusion when the leader of an organization has some knowledge and experience with disability rights issues; then change, while not necessarily easy, can be much smoother and less disruptive. But such people are hard to find.

To this day I still wonder about Claudia's notion that disability was the hardest issue for her organization to address. I regret not pushing her for an explanation. Maybe I thought I knew at least some of the reasons, such as that for this or any group of feminists invested in seeing themselves as strong, competent, and independent, disabled women, stereotypically viewed as needy and dependent, stirred up anxieties about their own dependency needs, especially as they age. Or perhaps they felt resentful that they would have to take care of their disabled sisters, as they have had to care for sick, aging, or otherwise dependent family members. Or maybe the presence of disabled women precipitated these women's doubts about the intactness of their own bodies or their fears of vulnerability or reinforced stereotypes of women as victims. Or, more mundanely, perhaps they were afraid that accommodating disabled women would be expensive, draining limited funds and resources.

Now, some fifteen years later (and thirty-plus years since I first began pushing my way into the women's movement), feminists have become more inclusive. Virtually every women's conference addresses disabled women's issues in at least a few sessions, and a small number of well-known women's organizations have sponsored entire conferences on disability. Yet few disabled women serve on governing boards or in leadership positions in mainstream women's groups, and those who do are often "the first and only." Even today, disabled women are more likely to be included out of obligation than out of appreciation of the contribution they can make. They are not seen as a rich source of diversity. The welcome mat is not yet out.

42. Disabled Women's Community

In the 1980s I was part of a small cadre of disabled women around the country whose mission was to raise awareness that disabled women faced double discrimination based on disability *and* gender. We insisted that sexism was alive and well in the disability community; this was news to the nondisabled world, which tended to view disabled people as genderless. Members of our small but loud activist group were among the "founding mothers" of the U.S. disabled women's movement that would gain momentum and visibility in the 1990s in preparation for the 1995 Fourth World Conference on Women in Beijing. Most of us began our work independently and in isolation. Some of us, for example, started groundbreaking programs that combined gender and disability equity issues; others became the sole advocate for disabled women's issues at a women's or disability conference, well before the women's movement had any consciousness of disability or the disability movement had any consciousness of gender. Not that either the women's or disability movement is overly welcoming of disabled women's issues even today, but at that time our issues and contributions were completely overlooked.

Little by little, we began meeting one another—at project directors' meetings sponsored by the funders of our programs or at disability-related gatherings. We had much in common—all about the same age (late twenties, early thirties), white, middle class, most with mobility disabilities, and all tired of being the sole voice for disabled women and girls. We quickly discovered that even two of us together at the same meeting could make far more of a ruckus than one.

If I'm honest, I'd have to say that as isolated as I felt working by myself on gender and disability projects like my mentoring program for disabled girls, and as eager as I was for camaraderie, I was initially ambivalent about becoming part of a disabled women's community. My ambivalence resulted to some extent from my upbringing as the only disabled person in my family, school, and neighborhood. Part of my identity was based on being "the only one." This often made me feel like a freak, but it also granted me a special status, particularly when I found that through my presence, I could break down at least some of people's negative assumptions about disability and gain a modicum of acceptance in the nondisabled world. In a society that privileges able-bodiedness, being accepted with or despite my disability seemed like an achievement. To win nondisabled people over despite my differences and then, when I became an activist, to use my acceptance to advocate for other disabled people became an important role and source of pride in my life. Thinking back on it now, that acceptance, that inclusion in the nondisabled world was more often conditional than complete, but particularly in my young adulthood, my expectations were fairly low. I was appreciative of being accepted even marginally; marginality was far better than rejection. Fortunately or unfortunately, my tolerance for marginality has lessened as I've grown older. But that is another story that I have described elsewhere.

Within a group of disabled women, my "only one" status was gone, and its absence raised complex identity issues for me. Not only was I no longer unique; other disabled women served as mirrors, mirrors that at times seemed distorted and thus frightening. Sometimes, looking at the bodies of other disabled women evoked my worst fears of what I might look like to the outside world. I suddenly saw myself through the eyes of those disgust-filled strangers that I so frequently encountered in my daily life, causing me to want to flee or dissociate myself. Such feelings contributed to my ambivalence during my early encounters with other disabled women activists. But the allure of belonging and connectedness had its own power.

Perhaps the most striking example of the deliciousness of community occurred in the early 1990s, at a federally sponsored three-day conference on health-care issues of women with disabilities; its goal was the development of a research agenda on disabled women's health. About a dozen of us "founding mothers" were invited as panel participants in a series of workshops at the conference. Although we had been asked to be speakers, we had been given little part in organizing the conference and hence had little control over its content or focus. Medical and research types, largely nondisabled, were the prime organizers of the conference, along with a few token disabled women who were not particularly political and had little involvement in the emerging disabled women's movement. The audience was largely nondisabled research, government, and medical professionals rather than members of the disability community. The conference was grounded far too much in the view of disability as a biological and medical fact rather than social and political phenomenon, with a strong emphasis on fixing or managing the patient's "damaged" body rather than empowering disabled women to have greater control over their bodies.

As soon as the conference began, the power dynamics became obvious, and many of the activist disabled women began to feel uneasy. Slowly but surely during that first day, we started gravitating toward each other. Our connection started with nonverbal cues, eye contact from those of us sitting in disparate sections of the room, each of us with perplexed, distressed faces mirroring one another.

This was the first government-sponsored event on health and disability that had focused specifically on women. Much of the research on health and medical issues of people with disabilities involved male subjects, particularly male war veterans. For example, the desire to help men disabled in combat return to a productive (and reproductive) life motivated the initial studies of sexuality and disability. Of course, the male focus in medical research is not unique to the disability community. But thanks in large part to the women's movement, there has been increasing focus on researching and addressing the health-care needs of women—that is, of nondisabled women. The interest in disabled women's health care has emerged far more slowly. This conference was the first public statement that gender mattered, that *women* mattered, when considering health care for people with disabilities. So for those of us who had been insisting for years that disability research needed to address gender issues, the fact that there was a conference on disabled women's health was in itself a great victory. Yet as disabled women activists, we were devastated and infuriated to be at this landmark event and to hear ourselves discussed as "the other" and, more specifically, "the defective other."

Our group began meeting to vent our fury and plot our strategies first in pairs, then in threes, and finally all together right outside the conference door. We demanded to meet the conference organizers, who couldn't quite comprehend what the problem was. In their minds, they had done the "right" thing. They had invited the "crippled girls" to speak. (This was our terminology, of course; the organizers knew the correct disability language, even if they didn't grasp its significance.) But for them this was a research conference that quite appropriately had been organized by researchers, not by the subjects of research. They did not feel responsible for the fact that most of the researchers on disabled women's health were nondisabled, nonactivist professionals, although they asked our advice on how to recruit more disabled women and men into the field of research. The organizers held a very traditional view of research and researchers; other government-organized health-research conferences unrelated to disability often similarly devalued the "populations" and "patients" being researched. But we were not comforted or appeased by the fact that such devaluation was equitable.

In addition to meeting with the conference organizers, our group repeatedly confronted speakers who used language and conceptualizations of the disability experience that were particularly derogatory. We got little satisfaction from either strategy. Perhaps the most healing aspects of our efforts occurred when we gathered to rant, applaud one another's work—the research and activism some of us were doing on health-care issues for disabled women, such as access to reproductive health care, dating and relationships, pregnancy, motherhood, and the barriers facing disabled lesbians, were quite extraordinary—and most important, simply be with one another and bathe in our collective presence. I had no desire to flee from those gatherings; I had rarely felt so welcomed at any other place in my life. I cannot fully explain what made the magic, but that deep connection was there, and I carry it with me now as I write.

I remember one incident that had a profound effect on me. Near the end of the conference we decided to have some type of leave-taking ritual before we all departed. One woman in the group proposed we hold hands, but another reminded us that this was an ableist tradition that served to exclude those of us who had limited use of our hands. And I remembered the many feminist activities I had attended where hand-holding was an aspect of building community—yet for me, with wiggling fingers that get increasingly wild with the containment of hand-holding, the request that we hold hands set me into a panic and set me apart. So when my disabled sister vetoed hand-holding as exclusionary and, by implication, understood my panic as no one else had, and as we found ourselves creating our own gesture of community that spoke more to who we were—touching the woman on either side of us in whatever way felt most comfortable—I knew that for at least that moment, I had found a home.

In addition to this experience, there have been for me other significant moments of communion as I have sought to find my way and my place in the disabled women's community. I recall, for example, the sense of connection and community that I felt when joining with my disabled sisters in a protest rally against the inaccessibility of the Disabled Women's Tent at the Fourth World Conference for Women in Beijing, a risky proposition since the Chinese government had banned rallies in the highly public location where we were marching. And I have fond memories of exchanging "You've got to be kidding" looks with a group of disabled women at another women's gathering when a nondisabled member of the audience made a patronizing "You're so inspirational" remark to a disabled woman who had just completed her presentation. Some of these moments have led to deep friendships with other disabled women with whom I have been able to be amazingly, deliciously, outrageously myself, without the caution, the self-restraint, and the self-silencing that has been characteristic of so much of my life. Not that my ambivalence has totally dissipated just yet. I still catch myself distancing and dissociating from women with disabilities who drool or whose speech is more impaired than mine, turning them into "the other," as nondisabled people have so often done to me. Nonetheless, I am grateful to have a home and feel increasingly at home in the disabled women's community.

43. The Story of Betty, Revisited

In 1984 I founded the Networking Project for Disabled Women and Girls, a mentoring project for disabled adolescent girls, which I describe in detail in a later chapter. At one of the kickoff events for the project, a conference that brought together for the first time the disabled girls I recruited for the project and the adult women with disabilities who agreed to be their mentors, I talked about my first serious encounter with a disabled person, Betty, a woman economist whom I worked for during the summer after I graduated from college. I described her profoundly positive effect on my life, explaining that she taught me about the value of mentoring and had served as the inspiration for the Networking Project. This was a story I would repeat dozens, if not hundreds, of times over the next several years to foster more mentoring opportunities for disabled girls. With enough repetitions, the story began to have a life of its own, so much so that it became hard for me to remember what my actual relationship was with Betty.

In the "official story," I claimed that because Betty was so successful in a man's career, antitrust economics, she helped me expand my career goals. That claim was not quite truthful, since I had never had difficulty envisioning myself having a career, and I gravitated toward male-dominated careers, such as math and economics, because I never felt very womanly. A much bigger issue for me during my adolescence was whether I would ever find a man to love and marry me. I had grown up with the stereotype that disabled women were unattractive, undesirable, and asexual. In "the story," I credited Betty with helping me challenge the stereotype. She was married, and, as I explained, her marriage planted the seeds of positive possibilities about my social potential that would ultimately enable me to begin dating. This was, at best, a partial truth. Betty's husband was a kind, gentle man but not terribly dashing or brilliant—not the kind of man that I, in my naïveté, thought a "real" (that is, nondisabled) woman would marry, since I assumed that nondisabled women had a wealth of choices for mates and that dashing and brilliant were better than down-to-earth and demure. I thought Betty had settled for a second-rate partner because she was disabled, just as I feared I would have to do if I were ever to marry. I would later learn much more both about the many wonderful qualities of Betty's husband and about the harsh realities of the dating/marriage game for many women, disabled or not.

My experiences with Betty that summer did not have as much impact on my sense of my own potential as I had claimed—at least not in the ways I stated. In some ways, Betty made a larger contribution to my life than what I explained to the girls at the conference. At that time I hadn't fully understood the profound nature of the gift she gave me and wouldn't necessarily have admitted its importance, even if I had understood what that gift was. Bluntly put, Betty was the first disabled person I had met who did not elicit in me feelings of shame and horror. I should mention that she had my disability, cerebral palsy, and it affected her in ways similar to how my disability affected me, although her speech was far clearer than mine. As I stated in the "official story," and this was true, when I met Betty at the job interview, it was like looking in the mirror. As I have frequently acknowledged, I have a difficult time looking in the mirror and confronting my disability-related differences. But looking at my mirror image through Betty became easier over time. I think that because she was smart, interesting, quirky, and creative and liked and admired me made the mirror friendlier and less frightening. Another way she affected me—or we affected each other—was that I, as a disabled woman, became a role model for her, a possibility that seemed inconceivable to me prior to meeting her. Betty had never spent time with another disabled person before she met me. She had grown up as "the only one," and her family was perhaps even more into denial, or at least normalizing, than mine. She told me that she did not even know the name of her disability until she applied for government job as a young woman; before being hired, she was required to get a medical exam that included a diagnosis of her "condition." So Betty, too, was taking a long, hard look in the mirror during that summer. Part of what she discovered in that mirror was that she had some abilities that she didn't realize. For example, she saw me using the photocopy machine and decided she could use it, too, whereas before then she had been convinced that, given her shakiness, it was beyond her capacity. So yes, Betty had a profound effect on my life (and to some degree, vice versa) but not in quite the ways I told those girls that day or audiences coast to coast for the next twenty years. She helped me tolerate other people with disabilities, and in the process I became more tolerant of myself. The road from tolerance to pride would be a lengthy one, and I've yet to go the full distance, but Betty's presence enabled me to take a major leap away from denial and self-hatred.

44. Listening to Myself

Listening to you, my sister with CP, I hear myself—the long pauses, syllables lost in one other, those gasps for air like a lynching in progress, last words ejected as the noose tightens.

Hearing as an outsider a voice like mine, I grasp the agony of misunderstanding: deathly illness, drunken stupor, dumbbell, "retard." Let the freak show begin.

Yet, after we spend time together over a glass or two of chardonnay, slowing me down, fogging over my judgments about you (and my being seen with you), your syllables start to coalesce into words that interest me—not that I agree with them all, mind you, and not that I understand them all, so will you please repeat and this time slowly, damn you! Did anyone ever tell you that you have a weird disability accent that's hard to grasp, weirder even than mine?

And you just become one of my many pain-in-the-ass friends with whom I have communication problems sans diagnoses unless you count neurotic.

45. Activist Sisters

Coming Out with Company

Roberta Galler and I met in the mid-1970s at a rowdy meeting of a local disability rights organization, the first meeting of this type that either of us had attended. Although we had both been disabled for decades—Roberta had had polio when she was ten and now walked with a crutch, and I had had cerebral palsy since birth—we were both at the beginning stages of acknowledging our disability status. Being in a room where everyone had a disability—also a first for both of us—would have been overwhelming enough in our struggle to claim the part of ourselves that had been disavowed all of our lives, but seeing these people yell and scream at each other and in some cases exhibit what seemed to be odd, inappropriate behavior was more than either of us could bear. Surely we were not like "them," each of us privately thought. And because we saw each other as one of the few calm, "normal"-looking people in the room, we gravitated toward each other and compared notes. What we discovered, in addition to our mutual discomfort with what was going on at the meeting, was that we both had social work degrees and were currently enrolled in advanced psychotherapy training programs with the hope of starting private practices as psychotherapists. While it was our relative calmness and similar career goals that initially drew us together, what really bound us during the initial years of a friendship that has lasted more than thirty-five years was our ability to share our fears and feelings of liberation about "coming out" disabled. We confessed our own discomfort at being with a group of disabled people and experiencing those with the most visible disabilities as frightening, distorted mirrors. "Oh no, I'm not like them," we admitted feeling. At the same time, we could acknowledge that being in such a group was a relief since we were no longer "the only one," compelled to hide our differences and our disability-related needs. We talked about nondisabled friends who had accepted our views of ourselves as nondisabled and were now annoyed when we acknowledged having limitations and needed help. "When did you become disabled?" they would ask. We talked about our growing sense of pride in asking for the help we needed. As Roberta stated so succinctly on behalf of both of us, "I used to congratulate myself for refusing help despite my needs. Now I congratulate myself for asking for precisely what I need." Over the years Roberta and I have often reminisced about our first meeting and laughed at our collective misdiagnoses of many of the people we met who later became friends and taught us, among other things, how to be outrageously "out."

Refusal to Be Silenced

I met Bobbi Linn in the 1970s at one of the many disability-related gatherings I had been attending at the time, ostensibly to drum up business for my budding psychotherapy practice but in reality to increase my tolerance for people with disabilities—that is, for myself. I was attempting to come out of the closet without even knowing that was what I was doing. Bobbi was one of the first people with cerebral palsy I met whose level of disability was similar to mine. Most of the other people with cerebral palsy that I had encountered were more significantly disabled, with mannerisms—drooling, incomprehensive (to me) speech, odd-looking body parts—that brought out my worst fears about myself. But Bobbi was, well, like me: She was appealing, with a relatively "normal"-looking body; her somewhat off-balance gait, her facial grimacing, and her not-always-but-usually-comprehensible speech patterns all resembled mine. Actually, when we met, I prided myself in thinking that my speech was more comprehensible than hers, which made me feel superior; I was still at the point where I needed to feel superior to—that is, less disabled than—others. Over time I was not so sure which of us had clearer speech; in fact, it no longer mattered. I suppose meeting Bobbi was so important because she so unabashedly, unapologetically acknowledged her disability. I could not imagine having such pride in my disability identity. I asked her at our first meeting whether her speech disability ever silenced her or made her choose to be sparse with her words. She laughed, explaining that nothing and nobody could ever silence her. She insisted that if people grew impatient or tried to disregard her, because they didn't understand her speech, that was too damn bad. Their impatience was their problem, not hers. Oh, how I loved hearing those words, even though I didn't yet believe her (and still don't, at least not 100 percent). She gave me something to hope for.

Watershed Moments

I didn't know Anna Fay well, although we had met many times and she had decided to replicate my mentoring project for disabled girls in Yonkers, New York, a city north of Manhattan, where she ran a disability rights organization. I knew she had been a leader in the disability rights movement both locally and nationally since the 1970s, but I didn't know the specifics of what she had done. Now I would get to hear her story, since I had been asked to interview her for the Disability Rights and Independent Living Movement Collection of oral histories and archives, a project of the Bancroft Library and its Regional Oral History Office at the University of California, Berkeley.

While I was fascinated by so much of Anna's story—I've always loved hearing people's stories, which was one factor in my decision to become a psychotherapist—and deeply impressed by her many contributions to disability rights, I was particularly transfixed by what she described as her "watershed moments." These were incidents that transformed her from a person who was shy and apologetic about her disability status to a strong, proud disability rights activist. For example, she told me during one of our informal conversations after the interview, "In the 1970s I was involved in organizing a protest that totally changed my image of myself. There was a gasoline shortage, and to save gas, the New York City government put severe restrictions on the use of private cars and vans. Certain groups were exempt—but not people with disabilities, even though there was no accessible transportation at that time. The disability community got outraged and decided to organize a demonstration. I was one of the key organizers, even though I had never done such a thing before, but my anger propelled me, and working with other disabled people energized me. I can still remember that moment being in the street with hoards of people. I was almost euphoric. Partly it was the collective energy. But it was also the sense that 'I helped to make this happen, and I'm here telling the world that I'm as good as anyone else. . . . You'll hear me, damn it! You'll hear me!'"

Her descriptions of these important incidents in her life were moving and meaningful, in part because they gave me the language to understand my own watershed moment, which I shared with her. While I was training to become a psychotherapist, the training institute terminated me, insisting that I was not suited to become a psychotherapist because my disability was too "traumatic" for patients to handle. After getting over my initial shock, I began meeting with other psychotherapists and discovered that many had faced similar discrimination. So one evening I, the woman who had been in the closet about being disabled for much of her life, found myself standing in front of a room of disabled therapists, organizing a set of activities—the formation of an organization and a national conference—to proclaim and protest our collective injustice. I was out there, claiming disability as a valid, vibrant part of myself, and I could no longer retreat.

I had known that this experience had been transformative, but hearing how Anna understood her own experiences put mine in a broader context, as though I had gone through an important rite of passage in joining the disability community.

Damaged Goods

I had set up a lunch date with Nadina LaSpina to see if I could coax her to moderate an event I was planning for Women's History Month 2003, a panel of disabled women writers reading their work. We had never spent time alone together before, but I had seen her at numerous disability events. A disability rights activist for decades, she was out protesting when I was barely out of the closet and was arrested dozens, if not hundreds, of times for her activism. She was also a strong advocate for disability culture and taught a course at the New School. We agreed to meet at La Lupe, a wheelchair-accessible restaurant in Greenwich Village, where we both lived.

Fairly early into our conversation, I discovered that Nadina was working on a memoir and would much prefer to be a reader than a moderator at the Women's History Month event. Without hesitation, I invited Nadina to read, knowing that her work would reflect a civil rights rather than the charity/tragedy model of disability. The business of our lunch finished, we began talking about our lives, moving beyond what we had both heard through the grapevine about each other. Our childhood stories quickly bound us together. While they differed in specifics, there was much common ground: our parents' hopes that with enough rehabilitation and hard work we would become "normal" or "cured" and, when those hopes were dashed, our parents' doubts that we would ever marry or have children because what man would want us? We talked in shorthand so immediately did we grasp each other's experiences of being perceived as damaged goods. We were also quick to acknowledge that getting involved with the disability rights movement ultimately saved us from that damaged self-perception, although we each admitted that we were not entirely free of it, that at times it came back to haunt us. I was grateful for being seen and known so quickly; we were fast friends on the road to becoming best friends.

Tell It Like It Is

I met Corbett O'Toole in the early 1980s at a groundbreaking conference designed to promote educational equity for girls and young women with disabilities. Although she gave a marvelous speech, I remember most strongly her sitting with a group of adolescent girls with disabilities, providing them with very explicit information about sex—the kind of information that they were longing to have but no one would tell them. I listened closely, because although I was more than twice, and in some cases, three times the age of any girl there, my knowledge of sex was only slightly better than theirs, and, unlike some of them, I had no firsthand sexual experience. However, I learned from Corbett far more about how to have the courage to speak out about taboo topics than how to have sex (in fifty-plus different positions). Even if I had Corbett's knowledge about sex and disability, I would have been hesitant to be so frank with the girls for fear that their parents, the conference organizers, or some other authority figure would be appalled and stop me. But Corbett was fearless. As I would learn over the years, this was quintessential Corbett. Whenever we were at a conference or even a social gathering and she had something controversial to say, she would not hesitate to speak up. "I don't care if you're broke; you must provide scholarships so disabled women can attend, and sign language interpreters, and attendant services," she said to the organizers of a mainstream women's conference who thought they were doing enough by picking a conference site that was wheelchair accessible. "So where are the queers on the keynote panel?" she barked at the disabled women who were organizing a conference on disabled women's sexuality and thought they had done enough by having a lesbian lead one of the workshops. And I remember the day she called me to say that she was organizing a group meeting with the editor of a major feminist magazine to protest a recent article written by a disabled woman that presented a negative slant on disability, and did I want to come? I, a coward about challenging such an important feminist institution, declined, but Corbett, accompanied by several other disabled women, had her say. Over the next few years, as I encountered repeated difficulties getting feminist institutions to embrace disability, I regretted that decision and my own inability to be more outspoken and fearless like Corbett. But she was a profound influence despite my fears. When I started my mentoring project for disabled adolescent girls and began to have conversations about sex, I felt her presence and told the truth—or at least as much as I knew, with stacks of explicit books at my side to fill in the rest.

Laughter in the Ladies Room

Simi Linton and I were laughing hysterically in the ladies room near the hospital auditorium, reflecting on the absurdity and stupidity of some of the medical staff's responses to our presentation on sexuality and disability. We had been doing this type of dog-and-pony show together for more than a year, trying to convince health-care providers that disabled people were as horny as everyone else and needed information about sexuality. Members of our audiences were invariably incredulous. "Isn't your vagina too dry for sex? I mean, surely you don't find sex pleasurable, and why would any man want to stick his penis in there?" a young male intern asked Simi, who has a spinal cord injury. "Lubricants, you know about those?" Simi began, trying to craft her response so it was not too hostile or sarcastic, all the time avoiding looking at me so we didn't crack up. "Harilyn, what a tragedy. You're such a pretty girl. You could have had any man," a nurse commented in total earnestness. I caught Simi's eye, and we shared an "oy vey" look, giving me a moment to temper my rage so I could respond coherently, albeit forcefully: "I've had a pretty active sex life in recent years, so there's nothing tragic about my life except other people's negative [i.e., stupid] assumptions." Being bombarded by such comments would be deadly if either one of us were doing this gig alone, but together we survived, if not thrived, by exchanging looks, laughter, and the shared knowledge that the world is dysfunctional and disturbed, not us.

46. Toilet Troubles

Beijing 1995, the Fourth World Conference on Women, bringing together a larger turnout of disabled women than at any prior international women's conference. Shitting and pissing. The great equalizer. In the hole. Except if you can't squat. A few quasi-accessible toilets for those of us with disabilities who, according to the views of the Chinese government, couldn't or shouldn't be out in public but were. Guiltily, I made my way toward one of those "special" toilets. I could squat, but my rear, abandoned by shaky legs, had wiped more than one filthy floor. Finally I had had enough, determined to claim one of the few privileges of being disabled at this conference. The toilet police—two hefty Chinese women assigned to catch the able-bodied cheaters—did not initially agree. They eyed me cautiously, curiously, assessing my every movement, ready to block my path. At last, they stepped aside, letting me enter. I was relieved, as was my bladder. Another reason to proudly claim my disability identity.

47. My Mentoring Project

My adolescence was probably the worst time of my life. In addition to the usual stresses of bodily changes, I was dealing, or not dealing, with disability-related physical differences that set me apart from peers in ways that were more marked than when I was younger. The dating scene, which preoccupied many of my friends, seemed beyond my grasp. Who would want me? The prospect of getting rid of "those pesky parents" by leaving home to go away to college or, as some of my friends joked, running away from home, terrified me. How could I leave my mother? I dealt with my stress by denying my differences along with my adolescent desires and by focusing on my schoolwork, which provided an escape.

About thirty years ago, a dear friend and social work colleague, Linda Nessel, and I were sharing our adolescent experiences, sparked by her description of some of the escapades of her adolescent children. As I was relating some of my horrific feelings and experiences from that time—and the absence of anyone to share them with—Linda, whose life work was program development for youth, proposed that I start a mentoring program for adolescent girls with disabilities that would provide them with the support I had lacked. She suggested that I pitch the program to the YWCA of the City of New York, where she worked, an agency known for its innovative programming for women and girls. Although I had serious doubts about my capacity to help girls with disabilities through their adolescence given that I had barely survived my own, Linda was convincing.

In 1984, after madly scrambling for funding, I started the Networking Project for Disabled Women and Girls, a mentoring program for adolescent girls with physical disabilities, at the Y. Its goal was to raise the girls' social, educational, and career aspirations by connecting them with a network of successful working women with disabilities who would serve as mentors and role models. My personal goal was to help girls feel more comfortable and accepting of their disabilities so that they would not have to deny or hide that part of themselves in order to feel "normal."

I knew from the outset that when I was an adolescent, I never would have joined the type of project I was creating; I was too invested in seeing myself as nondisabled to engage in any activity associated with disability. Many of the girls that I sought to recruit had a similar attitude. Even though they were in special education classes, they did not see themselves as disabled; it was one thing to be labeled by others and quite another to label yourself.

So how did I get the girls to come? The project initially appealed to them in a way that had not been part of its primary design. Whatever else it was going to be, the Networking Project was going to be a venue for typical adolescent hanging out and socializing that was otherwise denied to these teens. The girls saw attending sessions as a way to escape from their parents' house on the weekends, when the sessions were held. When I started the project, there was little accessible transportation in New York City. Many of the girls were stuck at home from Friday afternoon, when the school bus dropped them off, until Monday morning, when the bus picked them up again. A fair number lived in unsafe neighborhoods, which meant that they were not even allowed to hang out on the block with their friends. And they could not sneak out because many lived in inaccessible homes that required the assistance and permission of their families even to get to the street. The Networking Project, by offering door-to-door van and taxi service, was the perfect, and for many the only, escape.

Also, while my agenda for the girls was to engage them in serious conversation with older disabled women about education, careers, family life, and the like, the girls zeroed in on one topic of interest to every teenager, a topic that their parents and teachers often failed to mention, thinking that it was not relevant to these "atypical," "asexual" girls. When I went recruiting in their classrooms and their teachers were out of hearing range, I promised the girls that we would talk about sex. That was a big selling point!

Even with these motivating factors, the project was a hard sell, and I often dreaded the classroom recruitment visits. At that time I was still quite ill at ease with my own disability status and had little experience talking with teens who, as audiences go, were a formidable group, less polite and more likely to ask intrusive questions. Despite these barriers, I was able to recruit a core group of fifteen or twenty to join the project. Most were girls and young women of color between the ages of thirteen and twenty, with a range of physical disabilities.

Recruiting adult women with disabilities to serve as mentors was much easier. Because of my budding involvement in the disability rights movement, I knew a number of disabled women activists in New York City who were eager to serve. Many had never met adult women with disabilities while they were growing up, and, convinced that their own lives would have been better or easier if they had had disabled female role models, they were eager to take on the mentoring role. But my activist friends and colleagues were a fairly homogeneous group, reflecting the homogeneity of the disability rights movement of that time: white, middle class, college educated, in their thirties and forties. I was particularly eager to recruit disabled women of color since so many of the girls were African American and Latina but had great difficulty tracking them down despite extensive outreach to local companies and organizations. I am sure they were out there, but I apparently did not have the right networks—or enough perseverance. I did recruit a few disabled women of color as mentors, but not nearly enough.

Once I had developed the networks of women and girls, the question became how to bring them together. My original notion of mentoring was the traditional one of assigning each girl an adult woman who would spend time with and "mentor" her. The complexity of this model was brought home to me when I met with the administrator of the local chapter of Big Brothers and Big Sisters, a national organization that provides mentors to children in need of adult role models. She described the extensive process her agency used to screen the women interested in becoming Big Sisters, eliminating women not willing or able to make the necessary commitment to the program. For every hundred women who show up for the initial orientation session to become Big Sisters, only ten make the cut. Her description truly scared me. I had done no screening of mentors, welcoming every woman willing to join. Although I knew many of the mentors personally,

I really didn't know that much about their ability to relate to and work with girls. Indeed, I had some doubts about my own capacity to mentor teens, feeling I still needed mentoring myself.

My talk with the Big Sisters administrator disabused me of the notion of jumping into one-to-one mentoring too quickly. Group mentoring activities seemed a safer bet; through a group format, I could assess both the abilities of the mentors and the needs of the girls. Fortunately, when I was about to start developing the group mentoring activities, I hired an assistant, Linda Marks, who was the founder and director of a prominent feminist educational organization for women in New York City, the Crystal Quilt. She had extensive experience developing workshops and programs for women and some experience working with white, middle-class teens. Although she had limited knowledge of disability issues, she was a quick learner.

The core mentoring activity was theme-centered discussion groups at the Y in which the girls had the opportunity to ask the mentors questions about such topics as independent living ("How did you talk your mother into letting you move out of her house?"); independent travel ("Aren't you scared to travel on a bus by yourself?" [by the late 1980s, some of the buses were accessible]); and dating, sex, and parenting ("Can you really do 'it' if you're in a wheelchair?"). We also offered workshops designed to build essential survival skills—communicating with parents, self-advocacy, self-defense, problem solving, decision making, and so forth. What was striking in these discussion groups and workshops was the passivity and limited level of engagement that a considerable number of the girls displayed. For many, the highlight of the session appeared to be the time when we brought out the pizza or other snacks. Suddenly, they would come to life, eating and chitchatting with friends and sometimes with the mentors. In hindsight, I should have recognized that their behavior was typical of most teens and even more crucial for them since they had few opportunities to socialize with peers other than at school. But at the time, Linda and I kept worrying and wondering what we could do to light a fire under these girls.

We also had periodic mentoring activities outside the Y that involved less talking and more seeing and doing; the girls seemed somewhat more engaged in these. To counteract their limited career aspirations of fashion model, rock star, secretary, or "I don't know," we developed a group of worksite visits to women with disabilities who had interesting careers to see "one day in the life of" a neurochemist, a lawyer, a computer programmer, and people in other occupations. I was troubled that many of the careers we highlighted required higher educational levels than these girls were likely to attain. Most of the girls were receiving an inferior education in segregated special education classes and would obtain a high school diploma that most colleges would find unacceptable for admission. I stopped feeling so concerned when I became aware that many of the girls were impressed not by the kind of work the women did but by the fact that they worked at all. Until then, these girls had been convinced that after leaving school, they would have to return to their parents' home and do nothing.

To foster a sense of disability pride that would counter the shame and embarrassment that many girls displayed about their disabilities, we held a variety of cultural events highlighting the artistic and other achievements of disabled women. For example, in honor of Women's History Month, we organized a reading of disabled women's writings at a public library and had an event at one of the mentor's homes honoring a disabled woman, Carol Ann Roberson, who had just been appointed the director of what was then called the Mayor's Office for the Handicapped (now the Mayor's Office for People with Disabilities).

After more than a year, when Linda and I knew the women and girls fairly well, we decided to add a one-to-one mentoring component to the project. We used a variety of factors to match the women and girls: career interests, personality, communication style, disability type, race, ethnicity, socioeconomic group, geographic proximity, and our own sense of who might do well with whom. The pairs were asked to meet every four to six weeks in their homes, at restaurants, at movie theaters, or in any location that was convenient.

The one-to-one component was one of the least successful parts of the program. Fewer than half the mentor-mentee pairs kept meeting beyond a few months, although we had hoped for at least a one-year commitment; some pairs didn't survive beyond the first meeting. Some of the women acknowledged that given their work, family and other responsibilities, mentoring even on an infrequent basis was more than they could handle. Others described their frustration in encountering a silent teen at the end of the phone line and, more generally, their difficulties in engaging their mentee. The periodic training sessions we gave the mentors to provide information, build skills, and troubleshoot problems did not seem to help much. Probably we should have provided sessions for the girls themselves, who appeared somewhat uncertain about how to relate one-on-one to a woman who was not a mother, aunt, neighbor, or teacher. As one mentee so aptly put it, "What should I do with her?" Nonetheless, a few pairs were highly successful and kept meeting for years. What seemed to enable them to survive had nothing to do with the factors we matched them on but the mentor's ability to be a good listener and build trust and the pair's ability to spend time together doing activities that were fun.

As the project continued, I had increasing doubts about its ability to make a real difference for the girls. Few of the mentoring activities appeared to deeply engage them. Even if they had, in the face of the poverty, dangerous neighborhoods, inferior educational opportunities, racism, and gender and disability bias, providing them with disabled women mentors seemed like a Band-Aid approach when what was needed was major surgery—that is, core changes in the inequitable institutions and systems that were impacting and limiting these girls' lives.

A few years into the project, an outside evaluator who interviewed a large sample of girls found that several had become more independent. A few were now able to use public transportation, and one or two had moved into a college dorm or their own apartment. Some girls described their newfound ability to pursue careers that previously family and teachers had told them were out of the question. But I was not convinced. I had this sneaking suspicion that the major beneficiary of the Networking Project had been me.

At the time that I developed the Networking Project, there was great interest among those working with youth in mentoring programs, particularly for "high-risk" youth—adolescents at risk for dropping out of school, alcohol and drug abuse, unwanted pregnancies, and so forth. Similarly, those committed to women's issues were interested in gender-specific programming for girls, which included mentoring programs. Few such programs focused on disabled youth, much less disabled girls. The Networking Project was one of the first, if not the first, mentoring projects in the country specifically designed for disabled girls. Consequently, when conferences were held on youth development, mentoring, or girls' issues, the organizers, seeking to be inclusive in their conferences if not in their actual youth programs, often invited me to speak. During the six years that I directed the project, and for many years thereafter, I had numerous invitations to speak and gained a national reputation as the spokesperson for disabled girls.

My presentations described the needs and capacities of disabled girls and offered the Networking Project as a model for building on the strengths. While I had no doubt that I was doing important work in raising awareness of this large, diverse, largely invisible, greatly underserved group of girls, I had some serious reservations about presenting the Networking Project as an effective strategy to address the problems and barriers that they faced. Although I also advocated for the inclusion of disabled girls in all programs for youth and/or girls, I was concerned that the audience would view the Networking Project as "the" solution and replicate it widely. People in the audience appeared to love hearing about the project, perhaps because they viewed it as all-American, like motherhood and apple pie. And I had the fear that unintentionally, my talks might be reinforcing rather than challenging their stereotypes—something along the lines of "Disabled people should stick together and help their own kind" or, in its crudest form, "Cripples helping cripples. Isn't that nice?" Perhaps the project also got audience members off the hook in terms of figuring out how to include disabled girls in their own mentoring and other youth programs for "normal" kids; if disabled women took on the mentoring role, their programs would not have to.

I never expressed my reservations about the Networking Project publicly; that would not have been strategic given that the project was dependent on grants, and grant makers liked to hear about successes, not uncertainties. I needn't have worried about the widespread proliferation of the Networking Project model. A few committed disability organizations attempted to set up similar projects, which lasted no more than a couple of years because of lack of funding, but none of the nondisabled audience members were inspired to replicate the model. Unfortunately, I was not much more successful in encouraging mainstream youth or girls' programs to include girls with disabilities. Programs for youth are notoriously underfunded, and program administrators, sometimes rightly, often wrongly, viewed serving youth with disabilities as a costly proposition. In at least some cases, underlying their cost concerns were stereotypes of disabled girls as needy and totally different from nondisabled girls, requiring not only more staff time but also extensive staff training and expertise; in fact, as likely as not, open-mindedness and creativity would have been enough. My presentations were not sufficient to dispel their myths.

I left the Networking Project in 1990, as did my coworker Linda. By that time we had hired younger women with disabilities to work directly with the girls and mentors, including Katinka Neuhof and Angela Perez, each of whom was exceptionally gifted and would subsequently assume a leadership role; thus, Linda and I had been serving in largely administrative/supervisory roles. I had gotten involved in painting and wanted more time to develop my artistic skills. I continued, though, to serve as an advocate for disabled girls' issues, speaking at conferences and collaborating with others in the development of materials designed to help educators become more aware of the needs of disabled girls and their distinction from disabled boys. The Networking Project continued for more than fifteen years after I left, although it changed considerably under new leadership.

After leaving, occasionally, in my various roles as speaker, activist, and psychotherapist, I would encounter women who had been in the Networking Project when they were teens. As I talked with these former participants, I became most aware of the frustrations in their lives—their inability to find a job, their financial struggles living on Social Security benefits that barely covered their expenses, their difficulties finding a romantic partner, or, in some cases, the consequences of problematic relationships.

Talking with them confirmed for me my deepest fears about the Networking Project—that the contact with adult women with disabilities had done relatively little to improve their lives. Several of these women insisted that despite their frustrations, they were really okay, but I did not believe them.

Eventually, I decided to track down a group of former participants to determine what specifically the Networking Project did or did not do for them and to get their input on what else the project could have offered to make a greater difference in their lives. I talked with six women of color, by then in their late thirties and early forties, who had been in the Networking Project when I had been there; several continued after I left and worked with staff I had hired.

I found that I had underestimated the benefits of the project and had failed to grasp the kinds of experiences that had the greatest impact on them. Virtually all said that their involvement in the Networking Project was a key factor in enabling them to leave their parents' home and move into their own apartment. Given their parents' overprotectiveness and resistance to their moving out, their own self-doubts about whether they could manage on their own, and the limited stock of accessible housing in New York City, their ability to move out was a considerable achievement. The memory of my own gut-wrenching struggle to separate from my mother made their ability to leave home seem even more impressive. The women also attributed to the project such accomplishments as learning how to use public buses once these became accessible, applying for their first jobs, beginning to date, and more generally, according to their description, "doing adult woman things."

When I asked them to explain what parts of the project were most helpful, few mentioned the theme-centered discussions and workshops at the Y that made up the bulk of the project— except the discussions of dating, sex, and body image, which most described as invaluable. Rather, they emphasized the formal and informal outings to the mentors' homes or, more generally, out in the world, where they could do and see rather than "just talk." Several mentioned that visits to a mentor's or disabled staff member's home, where they saw totally accessible environments, nicely decorated rather than "hospital-like," confirmed for them that they could live independently, whereas before, having grown up in largely inaccessible homes, they seriously doubted that they could live on their own, at least not without their mother or an "overseer" nearby to help them. An opportunity to cook and eat lunch and clean up afterward in staff member Katinka Neuhof's apartment had offered further confirmation of their capacity to take care of themselves on their own (although Katinka confessed that her apartment was a wreck by the time the girls left). Occasionally meeting the mentor's or staff member's husband or partner or their children during these visits also planted seeds of possibilities.

Similarly, for some of the women who participated in the one-to-one mentoring component of the program, being invited to visit their mentors at home and share other aspects of a mentor's life—traveling in her car, visiting her where she worked, meeting her friends, going with her to the movies or out to eat—gave them a sense that they could have a good, interesting, enjoyable life when they got older.

Group outings with, or in some cases without, mentors also taught important lessons. Several of the women noted that going out to eat in restaurants, even to McDonald's, without their parents present and hovering made them feel grown up in ways they rarely had experienced before. For a few, the prospect of eating out motivated them to learn how to use the newly accessible public buses. Angela Perez, who succeeded me as director, had wisely offered to treat the girls to lunch at a restaurant but only if they could get to that restaurant by public transportation. The women recalled that they were terrified, but as one woman explained, "I was hungry, so I did it."

As I listened, I grasped the underlying principle that I sensed but didn't pay enough attention to when I was directing the project. Providing the girls with real-life experiences in the company of the mentors or staff with disabilities was far more meaningful than just talking or thinking about experiences or ideas. Offering experiences out in the world was important for all youth but more so for girls with disabilities because many of them led such isolated, sheltered lives, at least during the time I ran the project.

The mentors were more role models and friends than teachers, advisers, or counselors. That is what made the project a success. Simply by sharing a small part of their lives, these women had opened windows of opportunity for young people whose outlook had been unintentionally curbed by parents and other important adults in their lives.

Of course, the Networking Project was far from perfect. The women I spoke with wished certain issues that proved critical to their adult lives, such as managing finances; taking care of their health through eating right, exercise, and so forth; and balancing work and family responsibilities—important issues for all women that are compounded by disability—had been addressed, even if only in an experiential way. And they wished there had been a more careful selection of mentors, since they commented that some of the mentors in the project were not that helpful to them or hopeful about their own lives. Interestingly, they did not see the limited number of mentors of color as a significant problem. For many of them, the shared experience of disability was most essential in fostering their connection to the mentors.

The women I interviewed essentially told me that through the project, they learned that they could have disabilities and have full lives as women. While they didn't necessarily like having a disability, they discovered it needn't stop them from doing the things they wanted to do. When I expressed my concern that so many of them were unemployed and living on marginal budgets, they acknowledged that, on the one hand, as disabled women, they faced many more barriers to employment than nondisabled women, but, on the other, there were many unemployed nondisabled women, especially now. Leading a normal life didn't necessarily mean leading a problem-free life.

Through the Networking Project, these women had discovered that they could be disabled and have a normal life, whereas I had grown up thinking that being normal required being non-disabled, and hence I could have a normal life only by denying my disability. It was a profound difference in attitude. While I would have liked them (and everyone) to give up the mythical standard of normalcy, if through the Networking Project they were able to openly claim the part of themselves most stigmatized by society and still feel normal, that was, in my view, a significant accomplishment—one that I wish my adolescent self could have achieved.

48. Why Claim Disability?

Why do I want adolescent girls with disabilities, my younger sisters, coming of age decades behind me, to claim disability? Such young things, desperate to fit in, to look and be like everyone else. Surely I remember being thirteen, fifteen, nineteen, even twenty-five and thirty-one, denying, denouncing, dissing disability. And I remember all the pain, hiding, and hating that part of myself that meant no harm, that did the best it could, that faced double damnation—from the world and from me, its most punitive enemy.

If only I could spare them that self-hatred, secrecy, silence—help them see that there is nothing wrong with who they are, as they are, disability and all, that they can have a satisfying life with their disability, not despite it. Too much to expect from young girls who feel they must hide so much of themselves to get through their lives. Maybe time is the only teacher.

But oh, how I would like to save them time so they could get on with the real work of claiming space and a place for themselves, of demanding that the world embrace all of them.

49. Broken Silences

I will not be silent or silenced. The restraint, the confinement, makes my brain explode. Silence offers no protection from danger. Of what have I been afraid? To speak could mean rejection, pain, death. Death is the final silence. I am going to die sooner or later. Silence will not protect me.

You are never whole if you are silent. We do not speak for fear of scrutiny, stigma, or suffering. But we have already faced such injustices despite our silence. We honor fear more than our own voices. When the words of women are waiting, wanting to be heard, we must do all we can to find them, free them.

It is not our differences that immobilize us but silence. And there are so many silences to be broken.

50. Eulogy for My Nondisabled Self

You have served me well even if you were an illusive companion. When I was a child, you assured me I was okay. You helped me forget about the stares, the stupid questions, the calls to welcome Jesus into my life, an unlikely prospect for a nice Jewish girl, disabled or not.

You kept me company amid that desperate loneliness of being the only one in my family, community, universe, assuring me I was like everyone else, "normal," not "special," that fucking euphemism for not quite human.

But dear nondisabled self, you unwittingly harmed me, leaving me unprotected, without tools to fight the "normal police."

You see, when I encountered a mirror, I was shocked and discombobulated by what I saw: that loopy, lopsided walk; those darting, dancing shoulders; those wandering, wiggly fingers; that goofy, gimpy smile. "Who is that freak?" I wondered, before the horror of recognition set in.

When others called me disabled, handicapped, crippled, spaz, retard—need I go on?—my tongue became paralyzed; you should pardon my French. I could only slink away in shame instead of killing them softly with my words of pride about who I was—and was not.

So, dear nondisabled self, I've discovered your secret. You are as confused and conflicted about my disability as everyone else, a bona fide member of that normalcy brigade. And while I could try to coax you, cajole you, change you, better you should depart quietly, peacefully, with my thanks.

My mother thanks you; my father thanks you. You followed their commands to perfection. They thought you could save me—or at least save them and their "normal" world. You made them proud, but now they're gone. So get out now—and forever!

51. Eulogy for My Freakish Self

You have been lurking in the background of my soul all my life. You have leapt out at moments of triumph—"Don't get too happy!"—and delighted in my failures—"I told you so!" You have always threatened to reveal yourself to those who dared to love me.

I don't know how you came to be, dear freakish self. Perhaps everyone stores the seeds of a scary creature like you. But you had fertile ground in which to grow. A sea of stares seeping in, permeating, overflowing with dismay, disgust, despair, damnation, served as your amniotic fluid, your food, your shelter, your inspiration.

And all those questions, comments, jokes, torturous teases spurred you on: "What's wrong with you?" "Is it catching?" "Does it hurt?" "Are you drunk, dying, a spaz, a retard, a whacko, perhaps?" "Have you tried surgery, therapy, drugs, Jesus?"

But no matter how you came to be, you're here—unless you can be excavated, desecrated, exorcised. Who should preside? A rabbi? A priest? A minister? A mullah? I fear that those I know would rather be your ally than your executioner. Cripples don't fare well in most holy books or hearts.

My feisty mother might take you on. But she, too, harbored freakish fears, her flabby body not quite right for male delights. So even she might condone rather than condemn you.

This ghoulish task is mine. So how shall we begin? A quiet room, low lights, curtains drawn, two chairs across from one another. Oh no! Not therapy—not quite, not yet. Some quiet moments, some grieving, some sense of loss.

The task of letting the freak go will not be easy—no longer hating it, blaming it, hiding behind it when someone treats me badly or speaks some truth I refuse to hear or when I get angry at myself for believing the mirror or those stares.

Ah, dear freakish self, you have been not only a curse but also a companion, and I will miss you. But it is time for me to claim who I am, me, and not an illusion.

52. Ode to My Disabled Self

I suppose I should be grateful that you, dear body, function as well as you do. I could have been "much more badly handicapped," to quote my mother, who herself claimed gratitude for all you could do but also felt greed, wanting you to minimize, normalize, and sanitize away all outward signs of bodily limitations. I did, too, if I'm honest. No, I did one better, pretending for the longest time that you were perfect, normal, nondisabled.

That didn't stop me from fighting for the rights of bodies that looked like you or were "worse off, more crippled," as my mother would say (oh my, our mothers' words haunt us forever). I joined the disability community with pride but for the longest time remained an outsider, at least in my mind. "Oh no, I'm not really one of them."

But you were patient, accepting my denial, continuing to walk lopsidedly, with toes that touched, tripped, teased one another, and to talk haltingly, with words that slip-slided and slurred, being your own palsied self, waiting for me to wake up, grow up, shape up, shut down that Madison Avenue mirage lurking in my head and replace it with the truth of who I am, who we are.

All right, I concede. You, dear body of mine, are in perpetual motion: Your walk is crooked; your speech is garbled; you're a mess—not who I want to be. I wish you walked and talked and moved like every other body so I could wander the world unnoticed.

I've gone too far. I hear you screaming in my ear:

You want to kill me off, make me over simply to be invisible, boringly normal, indistinguishable from every body on the street? Have you no shame? No pride?

Dear body, stop mocking me. You know that looking "normal" would not sustain me for very long. Normalcy is the real illusion that every body, disabled or not, seeks without success.

Nice politically correct platitudes, but I'm lying. I do want to fit in, be normal—at least I think I do. Yet maybe my disabled body is not the issue and never has been, just a hook on which to hang my discontent about the job, the man, the life that got away.

I once had a psychotherapy patient who was jealous of my disabled body, insisting, "At least *you* have a concrete, bona fide, in-the-flesh reason to feel bad about yourself." But is that the real reason for self-hatred—or just a place to hide?

I suppose I should be grateful for what my body does imperfectly or otherwise. My walk, though clumsy, transports me, putting my fourth-floor walk-up, rent-stabilized apartment within reach. My speech, even when garbled, can express passion and hide ignorance, mine, enabling me to claim, "Oh, I never said that foolish thing. You misunderstood." My constant motion burns calories far more cheaply than a gym. And yes, I hate those stares. No way to talk myself out of that. But my body is not the culprit despite my mother's misconceptions. Ignorance, fear, nastiness, and prejudice are to blame, not my shaky bones. Besides, without those looks of confusion, disgust, and despair, I'd be out of a job. Who needs a disability activist in a perfect world?

You have been kind to me, dear body, more gracious than I have been to you. Of the two of us, you have more class, more wisdom. Let me embrace you as you have embraced me and sense your movements as signs of life, not limits.

Harilyn Rousso is a disability activist, feminist, psychotherapist, writer, and painter. She is the President of Disabilities Unlimited Consulting Services, founder of the Networking Project for Disabled Women and Girls, coeditor of *Double Jeopardy: Addressing Gender Equity in Special Education*, and author of *Disabled, Female, and Proud!*